My Gift to God

《——∞——》

A Journey of Raw Vulnerability
By Sarah McKinnis

My Gift to God: A Journey of Raw Vulnerability

Copyright ©2015 by Sarah McKinnis. All rights reserved.

All rights reserved. No portion of this book may be reproduced, stored in a retrieval system, or transmitted in any form or by any means-electronic, mechanical, photocopy, recording, scanning, or other-except for brief quotations in printed reviews, without the prior written permission of the author.

Some names and identifying details have been changed in this book to protect the privacy of individuals involved.

Author and cover photo by Arlyne VanHook Photography. Copyright ©2015 by Sarah McKinnis. All rights reserved.

Edited by Rebecca Howard
Formatted by Lori McClure

All scripture quotations, unless otherwise indicated, are taken from the Holy Bible, New International Version, ®NIV. ® Copyright ©1973, 1978, 1984 by International Bible Society, Used by permission of Zondervan Publishing House. All rights reserved worldwide.

ISBN: 978-1-932496-65-9

Printed in the United States of America
Printed at Dockins Graphics, Cleveland, Tennessee

TO MY ADAM,
Without you, the ending would be much different. Without God, who knows where we would be. But, with each other and with God, the story is beautiful. Thank you for being the one who has known me from the beginning. Thank you for being you, and thank you for being my favorite. I love you.

~ Contents ~

Prelude	vii
CHAPTER 1 Childhood Dreams	1
CHAPTER 2 The New Normal	11
CHAPTER 3 Teenage Frustration	23
CHAPTER 4 Responsibility	35
CHAPTER 5 Coming Out Alive	43
CHAPTER 6 Regaining Freedom	61
CHAPTER 7 God Speaks	69
CHAPTER 8 My Mammaw	75
CHAPTER 9 Successful Running	97
CHAPTER 10 The Devil's Intimate Blow	117
CHAPTER 11 Flirting	133
CHAPTER 12 Adam Visits	143
CHAPTER 13 Surgery	159
CHAPTER 14 Waking Up To Consequences	169
CHAPTER 15 Physical & Spiritual Recovery	185
CHAPTER 16 Coming Out of the Closet Backwards	209
CHAPTER 17 God's Promises Fulfilled	219
CHAPTER 18 What is Love?	229
Chapter 19 Becoming a Daughter	259
Chapter 20 Learning Forgiveness	279
Chapter 21 Spirit of a Warrior	287
Chapter 22 Restoration	297

Chapter 23 Encompassing Love	313
Chapter 24 Love Thy Neighbor	329
My Gift to God	335
A Note from Adam	339
Acknowledgments	341
~ Notes ~	347
<u>Teaching on Love through Ezekiel</u>	
About The Author	353

~ Prelude ~

«—∞—»

I have tasted the things of this world as if they were delicacies on a silver platter, taking as much as I wanted and trying new things as if all of the world belonged to me. The promises of this world would intrigue me. Bright and shiny prisms with glittering images would capture my eye and entangle my heart, allowing me just enough intrigue to convince me to turn the next corner to see what was next. Only to find when I passed the chandeliers and golden stairways I found myself in darkened hallways, lit with candles on velvet walls, with pimps standing outside each door, taking my hand and leading me into ecstasy. Passing rooms full of riches and jewels only to be handed off to the next pimp offering satin sheets and wine filled goblets. Dancing among the flickering candlelit hallways, searching for that which would satisfy my desires, only to find they were fleeting deceptions.

But still, I continued dancing in the hallways, sometimes running outside in the meadows to catch some fresh air before plunging back into my own little world of traipsing pathways. I felt free to come and go as I pleased until one day I found a small wooden door that so aroused my curiosity I could not pass by, and after taking the iron key that unlocked the metal flashing, I entered sheepishly, assessing each darkened corner to peer into the crevices before turning back to find the beautiful door had been shut and the key turned against me. Now, here I sat, amongst rock walls with shackles hanging in disdain, while hearing the distant cackles of my avengers down secluded hallways in a battle to their death.

Silent and alone, my heart was awakened, and as I heard the words to not initiate anything, I knew I must sit still. So I sat quiet, pensively at first. A small reading candle was lit, illuminating a little blue bible with a silver inscription, my name on it. There I sat and, as I began to open this book from long ago, a new candle would be lit daily, and small delicacies on wooden dishes would be left by the door providing nourishment for my soul. Each day brought more stories and more truth until one day I walked to the door to find there was no plate, but rather the door was slightly open, and I was allowed to walk the hallways from where I had entered with new light and new eyes.

My father met me there, leading me down the hallway of rooms and introducing me to my past through his eyes and revealing to me the truth to replace the lies that had entrapped me. I witnessed truths that had first been soaked in the devils tonic, the fine linens which were deceptively laced rags of disdain. We lingered in some rooms where I was angry, and I would scream from the depths of my soul at where I had been. I had to release pent up anger at believing unsupported doctrines which I had erected banners in my life upon. All the while my father stood there, allowing every emotion to come before comforting me with his love. We did not step one foot outside the door until resolution was written in my heart. Room after room we would pass through, and after our time inside, he would squeeze the wick with his fingers until it burned no more, causing the light from his truth to fill those rooms and tear down those walls. Lovingly, he was my escort into rooms of abuse, past relationships, childhood memories, and my decisions until we came to where the walls were no longer cemented. From there he led me into this beautiful, majestic garden where I would meet my bridegroom. My father had dressed me in a stunning lace gown, honeysuckles in my hair, and a veil covering my face. He introduced me to the one who would love me second only to Him, and as He placed my hand in my groom's, He lovingly betrothed me into the realization of His promises fulfilled.

My Gift to God is my story of how although I thought perfection was the only way to receive attention, feel significant or important, that truth being revealed this is actually a long standing lie, one in which I do not know where the history of it begins for everyone. In my life, it began at an early age. Circumstances beyond my control began weaving lies into my mind and heart. Eventually, memories became distorted truths, and consequences had no bearing on my heart or on my life. But, after years of pursuing my heart, God began to lovingly show me the truth of His grace and unending mercy. He began unraveling the lies and walking me through the memories of my youth so that I may come to know the truth. Although consequences had to be bared, His mighty grace held me through it all. It was in this time that Jesus met me and showed me that the greatest gift I could ever give my Father in Heaven was me, the real me, the ugly, complicated mess of a life that was entangling my heart. This is where I learned that my gift to God was also His gift to me. Truth and unending love.

This book is not just a story but a journey, in which raw vulnerability is laid open as a tempest full of truths that I wish were not mine. With this statement comes the truth that the story really belongs to my Heavenly Father, and that is why this is written with tears and released entrapment from my heart. No longer fearing retribution by people, but rather that light may be scattered where darkness attempts to prevail. There is absolutely no better understanding that can be captured than the love of the Father for each of His children. My hope is that by sharing candidly the paths I have run down seeking self-satisfaction and fulfilled happiness, you may understand that no perception by others or perception of yourself is worth the shackles that keep us locked away from truth being revealed. With that, my journey begins with you.

CHAPTER 1

Childhood Dreams
« —∞— »

GROWING UP IN A SMALL TOWN in east Tennessee, a community centered around Christianity with churches on every street corner, became the Bible belt influence of my childhood. My mother is a nurse who grew up as a preacher's daughter. My father grew up on a tobacco and dairy farm and did two tours in the Vietnam War as a helicopter gunman before coming back to the states and putting himself through college to become an accountant. Being in church literally every time the doors were open was normal existence for me, and so was the reality that I was a born and bred southern, daddy's girl. Quintessential at best, he was my idol and being outside, camping, riding horses, and all things farm life were my enjoyment. My parents were unwavering in their attempt to raise their only child in a harmonized, true American home full of God, family, and work. With their united, steadfast influence in my life, a young girl, strong-willed and independent in nature was being distinctly raised up.

My Gift to God

This instinctive, self-sufficient disposition cannot better be eloquently captured than in a memory of a day around the age of eight. My father and I were working in one of the large gardens behind our house which was shared with my grandmother and other family members that all lived in close proximity to each other, on roughly one hundred acres. His truck was out in the field, needing to be moved, and I was insistent with my daddy that I could move the truck myself. After much laughter on his part and stubborn discontent on my own, he said to me, "If you think you can do it, go ahead!" My grandmother, who was bent over picking beans, stood up, took her bonnet off her head and began to have a pure southern conniption fit, but he told her that I was so stubborn he was going to let me do it my way. I can tell you this was one example of many throughout my life that became a thread of truth to me.

That I could do anything and everything my way.

Carrying this attitude into adulthood, I can tell you some things turned out well with that uninhibited spirit, and others did not. That particular day, this little eight-year-old girl climbed up into her daddy's pickup truck, unable to sit on the seat and reach the gas pedal, so I stood. I turned the key in the ignition, shifted the truck into drive, and proceeded to drive straight into a pile of cinder blocks.

My daddy let me do it, just as my poppa in Heaven has let me do over and over again throughout my life when I was determined to do

Childhood Dreams

things my way. The truck was a little scratched up, but my daddy wanted me to learn a lesson. Looking back, I wish the effects of that long, hard lesson would have taken root that day.

With my Mother, I was a complete handful!

Being in the woods by myself was where I found copious amounts of peace and contentment. Escaping there often, I would sit very quietly and listen intently when my mother would commence yelling for me from the front porch to come inside. Perched as still as a mouse, careful not to disturb even a leaf or a limb, so she would be unable to find me, I would listen as the worry and concern in her voice would stringently intensify. Yet, unmoving, I would remain voiceless, until the willingness to come out of the woods was of my own desire. This, again, became another thread of reality throughout my teenage years and even well into adulthood.

Hiding from her, letting her scream for me, waiting her out for minutes or hours and, at one point, for even years.

One particular day, I came waltzing up out of the woods several hours after hearing her concern as she was watering flowers on the front porch. I climbed the steps, acting as if nothing was going on and began tormenting her. "Water me like you're watering the flowers, Momma!" After about twenty times of me badgering her, this was not an exaggeration, she turned around and dumped the newly filled water pitcher right over my head and proceeded to walk in the house, close the door, and leave me standing there! It was perfect. I got just what I had asked for. I think it is safe to say that, all of those days I spent hiding from her, I got just what I was not looking for as well later in life.

It all seemed pretty perfect, my life at the time, but just like many things, appearances do not always bring to light the shadows of reality in someone's home and life. My reality was about to receive a quick punch in the face when at nine years old my world turned upside down. Everything I knew to be true came rushing in as a pack of darkness. My daddy and I had been camping the night prior with friends and had come in from a trail ride on our horses. He decided to stop by the family barn to fix a couple of horseshoes while I was in my Uncle's house with some of my cousins. My memories of the next few moments were very scattered and did not make sense to me for decades. All I could remember was being in a frantic rush to get to him from the house, running breathlessly out towards the barn. I was in desperate need to get to him. For the longest time I did not understand why I was in such a rush to get to him, but I was.

When I reached the fence by the edge of the barn, I saw my daddy in between my two uncles, who were assisting him in walking, which he was unable to do by himself. I yelled for him urgently, "Daddy??!!" He turned around and stared at me with an expression that was not normal for him and some sort of gibberish came out of his mouth that I could not understand. With much perplexity and

Childhood Dreams

confusion, I watched my uncles turn him around and put him in the truck to take him back to our house to lay down, because they said he was not feeling well, while I stayed there at my uncle's.

A little later in the afternoon, I was down through the field at another Aunt and Uncle's home for a birthday party for my cousin, Breann. We were all outside when my Aunt Sherry came and told me that my mom was on the phone in the house, and she needed to speak to me. I went inside and my mother explained that my daddy was sick and being taken to the hospital, to which they said I threw down the phone and went running out of the house.

This running thing became another integral thread throughout my life as you will come to realize.

But this day, the running was significant. Everything I knew to be true that day was tossed into the air with absolutely no order for me to be able to understand. My daddy had never been sick, as far as I was concerned, and I knew something was desperately wrong.

The next days and weeks became increasingly foggy. At that time, a child was not permitted into ICU (Intensive Care Unit), no matter the circumstances, even with my mother being a nurse. I remember everyone telling me he was fine and that he was going to be okay, but this made no sense to me. If he was fine and he was going to be okay, then why was I sleeping on a couch in my aunt and uncle's living room? And, if he was fine, why could I not talk to him on the phone or see him?! One evening, while lying on the couch, staring at the brick fireplace in their living room, my mind was racing with all of the possibilities of what I knew to be factual, while trying to figure out why no one would explain the truth to me. The numerous doubts and inconsistencies made no reasonable sense. In that moment of questioning, was the first time in my life I ever heard God speak to my heart.

This peacefulness overtook my entire being as I heard the words, "Your daddy is okay."

It is unexplainable, even though, today, I remember that moment like it just occurred. The words did not create an excitement but rather an overwhelming sense of comfort. The only problem with hearing this was my expectation of "Okay" and God's words were at opposite ends of the spectrum. As it turned out, he suffered a massive cerebral hemorrhage and had a stroke. My aunt told me a few years ago that they attempted to let me talk to him on the phone one day, but I thought it was just another lie because it did not sound like him. Even more disconcerting than the phone call was the first time I actually was able to see him. I was so excited. Finally, I was going to be able to be in his presence and run into his arms so he could make me understand what had been going on and where he had been. I had so many questions to ask him, but more than that was just overwhelmed with excitement to be with him! Boy, was I in for a very rude awakening. I was completely unprepared and blindsided when he was wheeled into the room, sitting in a

Childhood Dreams

wheelchair, and I went to run and jump into his lap with much anticipation, but he could not hold me.

Not only could he not hold me, but he looked different. His eyes held considerable confusion and occupied unvoiced questions, which became identical to this little daddy's girl heart.

The days, weeks, and months after this brought continual changes, and my life seemed like a scattered box of nothingness.

Who was this man that was before me when he came home from the hospital? Always in a wheelchair with no words to say and eyes full of emotions he could not communicate.

We were trying to find a new normal with speech therapists and physical therapists coming to the house, learning to talk using pencil and paper instead of words. Yet maddening confusion entailed when his brain could not connect the dots with what he was trying to write or say with what actually came out. The stress in our home became something I had never known before. In addition to those adjustments were the financial restrictions my mother was now facing. As a nine-year-old, none of these things made sense. All I saw was that in a year's time our horses were sold, our house was sold, and my woods became city streets when we moved from the country house, into the city, into one of our rental homes. My dogs, not used to restrictive fences, could not stay in the city because they jumped the fence chasing neighbor kids, so they had to go back to the country, as well. The final blow was one year after the stroke.

My Gift to God

My mother sent me to Florida with some family friends, and when I came home, my daddy was living down the street in an apartment, and my parents had gotten divorced. There had been no explanation given and once again, no one was sharing the truth or preparing me for the events taking place.

It was at this point, I realized my life as I knew it and what I had hoped and dreamed would be restored, was lost to never return.

Again, my heart became broken.

The lack of communication to provide clarity to the changes that were transpiring within our family was devastating to me. Once again, I was left with numerous unanswered questions. Although my parent's marriage was not perfect prior to the stroke, the absence of being made to understand what was taking place only generated bitterness. It was not until later in life that I came to realize my mother was doing what she could to keep us all afloat. Instead, I witnessed her being the cause of all the change, and I began blaming her for all that was going wrong.

A thread of distrust and hatred began weaving its way around my heart with my mother, ever so tightly, that there was no room for compassion or love on my part towards her. She was attempting to protect me, but what she did not know at the time was that the need for protection had already expired in my heart. On the day my father had his strok, I ran breathlessly to him to reveal what had already been taken from me that day, and in the years prior.

Childhood Dreams

My innocence had been stolen, and I wanted the captor revealed that day.

Even to this day, they have never been revealed. Although I could say the devil is the captain with the master plan, his earthly cohorts remain nameless to everyone, except me and God.

For decades after the stroke, I would not have even told you there was such a thing taken from me because along with my father's words becoming silenced, my memories became bound up in the stress from it all. I remembered very few things for many years and could count on one hand what I recalled of the days and years preceding my father's stroke. It was as if one day they just magically disappeared.

In the next few years, dramatic changes continued to unfold. I became withdrawn and quiet, some would say contemplative, which I am even to this day. Listening to friends at school talk of their parents and memories of things they had experienced was challenging. I had no memories or stories to contribute other than, "I saw my dad last night and he was drunk again and still didn't have anything to say to me." Or, "My mom worked the night shift last night, and I haven't seen her or talked to her all day either." So, my thoughts turned inward and my trusting of others continued to falter even deeper.

CHAPTER 2

The New Normal

《 —∞— 》

THE NEXT FEW YEARS BECAME AN attempt to figure out what normal was for my life. There was no more camping, no more running through the acres of woods as freely as I wished, no more riding horses from daylight to dusk, no more. No more normalcy. My new normal became walking down a city street with a laundry basket to wash my daddy's laundry and clean his apartment during the week in an attempt to spend time with him, and then Saturday mornings we would eat breakfast at a local restaurant. That was the extent of the time I was now able to spend with this man who had been my entire world for nine years. My mom still took me to church every time the doors were open, but other than that, our relationship was already on a slippery slope. My memory of this time was of her becoming even more withdrawn and quiet than what was natural for her, while inside, I was still screaming for someone, anyone, to explain to me what was going on. Things had no order, circumstances unexplained to protect me or because I was a child, further tightened the weaving of distrust. Enrolled in a new school, family who were a daily part of my life prior to the stroke, started becoming strangers. Not knowing how to behave or how to externalize the uneasiness in my mind and emotions, it sent me into a manner of internalizing every thought and question I had, because of all that was left unanswered.

My new normal was a deafening silence from everywhere, except my mind, and there the devil began his manipulation into what truth was to me.

As the weeks progressed, each day took on an unwanted rhythm of its own:

School,

Home,

Walk to my dad's.

He was drinking.

Sit with the TV blaring while he drank, just to be near him.

Walk back up the street to home.

Escape to my room or try to play outside . . . but I was awkward and no longer fit in.

I was forgetting how to laugh, and I had cried until I no longer had tears. I learned how to cut off my emotions so I didn't have to feel, because feeling meant sadness would overcome my heart. No longer wanting to hurt, I would stand and talk to myself in the mirror because no one else was talking to me with any truth coming out of their mouths. So, truth became whatever I made it to be. I was

The New Normal

awkward not just to my family, but to schoolmates as well. Kids began making fun of my awkwardness, and again, this just sent me deeper into wanting to be alone.

Cindy, a girl who lived two houses down from me, and I began developing a quick friendship. She faced some physical challenges and because we were both viewed as peculiar by our schoolmates, we developed trust effortlessly as we realized we had no motivation to make fun of each other in a hurtful manner. We could laugh freely, and there was absolutely no pretense to worry about. Soon after this friendship began, however, she informed me that her and her parents were going to be moving soon, out of state.

I couldn't believe it!

Finally, I had found a friend who I could trust, who did not want anything from me, and now she was leaving.

I was convinced that my life would be over without this friendship, not dramatic in the least, I know!

So one afternoon, Cindy and I developed a brilliant plan that I would simply move with her and her family. My mom walked into my room the day they were loading their vehicles to leave. I had managed to pull a very large, red, vinyl suitcase with silver locks on it, out of the closet, packing it so full that the latches would not close. She asked what I was doing. With indignant confidence, I matter of factly explained I was running away and moving with Cindy to Illinois. She started laughing at me, which irritated me immensely, as I was still attempting to latch the suitcase. She then asked how I was planning to get there. I clarified to her our plan: I was taking one suitcase, putting it in their car, and riding with them to Illinois. Cindy and I were certain that her parents would not object. She then told me, with a smirk in her voice, "If you think that you can do that, go right ahead."

Finally securing the latches on the suitcase, I cumbersomely managed to stand it upright, even though it was half the size of me, grabbed the pull string and proceeded down the hall. Out the front door and down the street I went. It had to be quite hysterical if you could picture me pulling this suitcase down the middle of the road with it falling over every few feet and me stopping to try and set it back up with all of my strength. I am pretty certain my mom stood in the driveway and watched this episode transpire all the way down to Cindy's house, where once again my little hopes became crushed when I discovered that I would not be able to accompany my friend to Illinois.

With the continuation of these repeated disappointments, the belief that I was the only one I could depend on started developing and I was barely ten years old.

Today, I sometimes look at children around that age and think, "That was the age when I became an adult, in my mind." I wonder if there is comprehension of the influence that circumstances and events are having over that child. It is disheartening to realize that,

The New Normal

in certain situations, children are typically disregarded to the depths of acknowledgment and development present in their minds and hearts that will affect them the rest of their life, merely because they are young in age. These experiences in my life, wrote deep-rooted untruths in my heart and mind, which still, today, are being dismantled.

Accompanying the revelation of my own independence was an anger that began encroaching upon my heart and in my actions. Prior to my parents divorcing, but after moving into the city, there was a particular day that this little girl who wanted to talk to her daddy more than anything in the world, launched into action. Although it was not abnormal for my dad to drink prior to the stroke, being drunk on a daily basis, as his main activity for the day, was not normal. To me, this was just one more antagonist that kept us from being able to communicate and one which, physically, I could find a solution to. Each morning he would go to the store and buy a case of beer. By noon, he would be drunk. So one morning, I had had enough!

After he went to lie down after his daily beer run, I grabbed a chair from the kitchen table, pulled all of his newly purchased beer from the fridge, and proceeded to empty

Every

Single

Can

down the drain of the sink.

I thought I had found the perfect solution to my daddy talking to me in our newfound form of speaking. Finally, I would have his undivided attention, once again. So, I anxiously waited for him to wake up.

Much to my surprise, when he woke up and went to the refrigerator, the attention I received was not quite the conversation I was anticipating.

His anger, and my hurt, collided at that defining moment.

It was a moment in time that sometimes I tell with a comical twist, but during those minutes and the hours of that day, there was not an ounce of humor present.

I wanted my daddy!

I needed my daddy!

What I received was drunken anger, the first of many that became a relevant normalcy in our relationship.

About a year after my parents divorced, there was another instance of hurt and anger colliding, that was also a defining moment. I was a member of the Girl Scouts and we were having a Father/Daughter dinner. The event had been specifically planned so that all of the tables were individually set for just one daughter and one father with pretty little table cloths and vases with flowers in them. At home, we had each prepared meals our fathers would enjoy and delivered them to the school, where our dinner was being hosted.

The New Normal

After everything was set up, we then went home to dress in our Girl Scouts uniforms to return a little later with our fathers for our dinner date. I went home and fixed my hair just right, with my little cap, put on my little uniform so neat and perfect, knowing he would be proud of all of the badges I had worked so hard for. Reading over the speech I had worked on to give that night, I then anxiously waited for his arrival, to pick me up.

And I waited.

And I waited some more.

I began pacing in the driveway because we were going to be late. My mother began trying to fix it when it did not appear that he was going to show up, by calling my uncle to go with me.

But, my uncle was not my daddy!

I did not want anyone but my daddy. I had prepared the speech, for my daddy . . . the meal . . . the flowers . . . for my daddy.

I remember my mother pacing the floor in the kitchen, on the phone, not knowing what to do, while I sat in confusion.

How could he forget me? How could he not show up? So many questions!

To this day, I am unclear of how he arrived at the house or how we made it to the school. However, the one thing I do remember is he did show up and although we were late, we did go, but he had been drinking, and the proudness I expected from him, was lost on empty eyes. He was angry because he was being made to do something, and I was hurt, once again, because all in the world I wanted was to be his little girl again. To be the apple of his eye, for him to be proud of me, for him to tell me that he loved me. With these things being unaccomplished on a regular basis, the hurt turned into resounding anger. My new normal was unacceptable to me. So, the truth of not allowing hurt to overcome me, turned into closing myself down to feeling hurt and opening myself to what the devil was offering as protection, and that was anger.

Distrust, Anger, Hate, and Blame became my mantra. I would put on a happy face to try and get through the day, but at home, in the comfort of my room, alone, the devil would talk to me through the mirror telling me I was the only one I could depend on. Everything else was a pure, unadulterated lie. I had an alcoholic for a father, a mother who I blamed for everything going wrong, and my friends were really just people to get me through the day. I would be the good little girl to your face, but at night, the devil was telling me how evil I was and had me so utterly convinced, that I would literally look myself in the eyes and speak aloud that I must be the devil in disguise.

You may ask, "Well if you were in church every time the doors were open with your mom, where was God in all of this?" What I can tell you now, is that I do know there was a presence of protection, even though I did not recognize it then. I knew I had undeniably heard God's voice after my dad's stroke telling me he

The New Normal

was okay, but my distrust of God was even initiated at this time. Going to church simply became something I did. It was a part of my life, but it was not relationship based. More often than not, it had turned into just my mother and me going to the same church we had always attended. Once my dad was able to drive again, he started attending my aunt and uncle's church, even though his sole motivation was for God to heal him and restore him. I loved being able to go to church with my daddy and standing beside him singing songs from the hymnal, while holding his hand, conjured up enormous joy in my heart.

I remember the day I got saved.

We had been attending church together for several weeks, but my mom was not with us. I think she had worked third shift in the emergency room the night before. We were standing up and had been singing from the hymnal, after the message from the minister. I remember looking up at my daddy and seeing the hope in his eyes, and I wanted that so much!

I remember thinking, "If God can give him that hope that I haven't seen in so long, maybe I can get that hope too, and my daddy will be healed."

That was the day I let go of his hand, walked to the front of the church, and gave my heart to Jesus. I gave it in hopes for him, rather than for me, though. My prayer was innocent and truly seeking and I believed with all of my heart that he would be healed. But after

My Gift to God

many weeks and months passed, my dad started losing hope because he wanted to be healed quickly, on his time frame, and the drinking began to overtake everything else.

Along with his hope disappearing, mine began to follow into the abyss, also. The more things started disappearing that my dad worked so hard for, the more intensely the anger and drinking came into play for him. In that year after his stroke, I believe he and I both felt like spectators, watching the horses be sold, our house and land on the family farm being sold, and country roads turning into city streets. And when my dad's college diplomas arrived home in a box, taken off of the wall at his accounting practice, it seemed there we sat, and the hurt just kept piling up for both of us.

The dwindling hope I witnessed and the resoluteness of his reality setting in, influenced me deeply. I wanted him to hold on to the hope and to not give up. I wanted him to continue to take me to church and to go on drives in the country with the hopes we would once again be able to go horseback riding and camping again. That somehow, someway our life would return to what we knew. But, that was not the case. So when the instantaneous healing from Jesus did not manifest, the darkness became even thicker. The surface level, self-motivated faith was not, and is not, what God's healing is about. It is a very hard realization to come to terms with, knowing that all things are in God's time and not in our own. If we put our time frame on the promises we seek, we set ourselves up for

The New Normal

disappointment that can last a lifetime, if we let it. We can fall victim to it, or we can give it away and let God reveal to us in His time through grace, mercy, and love. It seems like a cliché, but actually, it is truth.

CHAPTER 3

Teenage Frustration

« —∞— »

AS THE YEARS PROGRESSED, I became increasingly clever at concealing my internal feelings while also attempting to be whom everyone thought I should be. My father's drinking continued to elevate to levels that ushered in disregard for what everyone else wanted, because he just wanted to not live in this newfound existence of reality he had found himself in. And my mother was endeavoring to provide for us better by returning to college to become a registered nurse. In the summer prior to my freshman year of high school, some very close friends of our family discussed with my mom the prospect of me coming to live with them for a year while she was working and finishing her studies.

To give more clarity to the relationship, my mom and both Ruth and Clarence had been friends since their teenage years and their daughter, Carol Lea, is barely two months older than I am. My mother was at her birth, and Ruth was at mine, and for as long as I can remember I would spend several weeks in the summertime with them. Even to this day, Carol Lea and I consider ourselves more like sisters, than friends, because we have known each other, literally, our entire lives.

This is a moment in time where I can definitively tell you God was interjecting into my life a sense of stability to a girl who was wavering on all accounts.

I lived with them in a small town in northeast TN, nearly two hundred miles away from my hometown, for one entire school year. This was beneficial for me, but it was also challenging. Once again, the surroundings I had become accustomed to changed and my first year of high school would be spent where the only person I knew, was Carol Lea. This was also a difficult adjustment for her, because we are both only children. I viewed this opportunity as a fresh start to recreate myself and arrived prepared to be the "good" girl by putting on the deceptiveness that had started to become natural for me. We lived, fought, and loved just like sisters and her friendship on this earth continues to be more impactful on my life than she will ever know. Clarence was, and still is, a pastor, so in essence I became a preacher's daughter for one year.

I am so thankful for that year with them, because God showed me what a Christian marriage looked like from the inside, and what a real prayer life looked like. Every morning we had prayer time before school. We ate breakfast and dinner together as a family, at the table. Sunday afternoons we had lunch together after morning services and then rested before church again in the evening.

Teenage Frustration

Clarence and Ruth took us on many hiking and traveling adventures and began teaching both of us how to drive a car. I felt, for once, I was a part of a normal family. Although we had our moments, as all families and siblings do, those transmitted a sense of normalcy into my life, also. I missed my family and friends, but it was countered with a joy of belonging. When it came time to leave, I was not ready to go back to what my normal was with my real mom and dad, but it was meant for me to return.

That summer was quite awkward, trying to reconnect with my close friends at home after being away for a year, so my sophomore year of high school was like entering a new atmosphere all over again. Coupling the re-entering into friendships in school with the introduction of teenage hormones was tremendously overpowering and frustrating that year. Whereas I had grown genuinely close in my relationship to God and with friends during the previous year, I felt like I was on an island all alone when I got back. Feeling disconnected from my schoolmates, friends, and the youth group of the church that I had grown up attending, I asked my mother if it would be possible to begin attending a church closer in town. Thinking it would be both more convenient for her and that it would usher in the opportunity to develop friendships with those who I saw on a more consistent basis, she agreed, as she was finishing up her final semesters of nursing school. With my friendships, this transition proved to be helpful, but the closeness I had felt in my relationship to God began to quickly and quietly disappear. My prayer time was no longer disciplined and something else started to materialize along this time, as well.

A solid friendship had developed between a girl named Jasmine and myself, and we became inseparable. Her home life was somewhat troubling and chaotic and we both sought protection with each other. The easiness with which our friendship progressed resonated because we did not have to keep any secrets from each other. And although we spoke of various occurrences from our younger years in code, there was nothing that was off limits between us.

One night, while she was at my house, I realized something that took me off guard.

Not only was this girl my friend, but I was developing feelings for her, and was awestruck by her beauty.

In that moment of comprehension, I looked myself in the mirror and said out loud to myself, that I loved her.

Being closer to her was what I desired, but I knew the nearness I desired was not right or acceptable! And the acknowledgment in that solitary instance ushered in the collision of my hormones and my past, and the devil began intruding and overtaking parts of me that are indescribable. She never knew of my feelings for her, outright, although there must have been some inclination because she began flirting and teasing me quite heavily. This messed with my mind and

Teenage Frustration

my heart, but more than that, I began remembering the day that I ran out to my daddy, when he was having his stroke.

Running from the house to the barn, I had just escaped a room where I had been involved with a female cousin, sexually. It had not just happened that day, however, it had been taking place for several years. The sexual abuse that had been occurring took on many different forms, but the predominant occurrence was what had just been happening. With the onslaught of those memories and the new verbal confession to myself, regarding Jasmine, it all left me befuddled.

The confusion that ensued was boggling to me.

How?!

Why?!

The memories flooded me daily and tormented me at night, to the point that I began looking at myself in the mirror and began calling myself the devil, daily.

If I was not the devil, then why?!

Why did those things happen?

Why did I have sex with my female cousin?

Why do I have these feelings for girls?

Why do I want to hold hands with only my female cousins, under a covering, so no one will see?

How did I even know what sex was at such a young age?

I must be the devil in disguise.

I am the devil in disguise!

Those were the thoughts the devil began to write on my heart as truth! I believed them, but I knew I must hide them.

I eventually started dating a guy in school who I liked, but more than anything, it was to suppress my inward desires. I needed a safety net. I needed to not feel these feelings. We became sexually active not long after my sixteenth birthday. Afterwards, I remember some of my friends talking about the pain they had experienced the first time they had sex, and for some the bleeding that had occurred. I could not relate to these details because they had not happened with me. Once again, I felt abnormal. Confirmation, once again, that I must be the devil because I am different than the others and they have no idea. To suppress these feelings and try to manipulate my thought processes proved to be impossible, so I created a new normalcy for myself.

I told people that he was my first love when actually she had been.

I told my friends he was my first kiss and first sexual partner when actually my cousin had been. Real truth became really no truth at all.

My truth, became again, whatever I made it to be at the time.

During these years, I was also introduced to a number of other things including drugs and alcohol, but I was determined to not try any of them and succeeded in that undertaking until well into my

Teenage Frustration

twenties. I became the "good girl" of my friends. Some of them would do drugs and drink while I was the one at the party that kept everything cleaned up or took care of those too far gone, mainly because I did not want to become what I saw my dad becoming as an alcoholic. I could divide out a quarter or dime bag of pot, but I refused to smoke it. In my mind, I was doing the right thing, because I did not want any possibility of becoming addicted to anything, in any way, at all. My mother and I were still in the midst of a very tumultuous and unhealthy relationship and I voiced my hatred of her without care who heard it. I still blamed her for all of the changes in my life; I even blamed her for my father's, now, absence in my life.

When I saw him, if I saw him, he was drunk and he showed no concern for my well-being, at all, at least not outwardly.

My home life felt like a joke with no father present and a mother whom I hated and who I wanted everyone else to hate also. Still, I wanted to appear "perfect" and "good" on the outside. My senior year in high school was filled with pretty much just trying to get away with whatever I could, under what I felt was the control of my mother. Instead of talking to me herself, she began talking to my youth group leader at the church and I felt she was just interfering. She also had people she worked with come and talk with me, or would take me to my grandfather or my godfather, who both happened to be ministers, and either leave me with them to talk or sit in judgment against me. This created a feeling of having nowhere that was safe to discuss what was really going on inside with me, without consequences. I had learned that she wanted me to confess to having sex, so my boyfriend could be charged with having sex with a minor, or statutory rape. So, I lied when asked about our relationship, although I really did not want to. She accused me of doing drugs, which I very self-righteously denied, and it was the truth, but again I was unwilling to indict my friends in the process.

Everything, for me began spiraling at this time.

My father was drinking so heavily that he did not even look like himself and indicated his intentions were to drink himself to death, because he no longer wanted to live. He began drinking and driving instead of just drinking at home and at some point moved from the apartment down the street, back to the country farm with my grandmother. Not long after being arrested by the police, for the second time, on drunk driving charges, he was sent to rehab in order to stay out of jail. I would go and visit and it was like seeing a different person, but he still had no desire to change or to live for that matter. He did his time there, got out and went right back to drinking and driving.

At one point, the fighting with my mother became so intense I decided I could take no more. Because I had threatened to leave and my associations with certain friends she did not approve of, she had a neighbor bolt the window shut so there could be no exit or entry from my bedroom. However, this particular day I was emphatic that the chaos of fighting and yelling had to end. As she locked the bedroom door while exiting my room, after one of our screaming bouts, I turned my stereo up to an acceptable level, threw some clothes in a bag from my closet, took a nail file and vigorously cut the edge of the screen frame out. After throwing the bag out of the window, I climbed up on my bed and hoisted myself over the windowsill, jumping to the ground to escape. With bleeding wrists, because I had not let go quick enough, I ran to my car, put it in neutral to back out of the driveway quietly, before my mother figured out what was going on. As I was backing into the street she came running out to stand in front of the car, so I threw it in reverse and backed all of the way up the road, determined to leave her standing there staring after me.

I had decided I wanted to stay with my daddy, but we were both in for a surprise when I arrived. I had become increasingly convinced that I was the only person I would ever be able to depend on, which furthered my distrust and skepticism of anyone who attempted to get too close to me. But, I thought I wanted to try and get close to him once more.

Not realizing, I really just wanted to be my daddy's little girl again.

One morning, much like when I was younger, I was attempting to get his attention and wanted him to talk to me. I was seventeen, and once again, trying to get some communication started. He had

My Gift to God

already been on his morning beer run; some things had not changed over the years, and he was reading the newspaper with the television blaring. I got up and turned the television down and he glared over the paper at me prior to turning the volume back up. I did this two more times, each time the stare was a little longer from him, telling me not to do it again with his eyes. But being the stubborn, obstinate person that I am, I got up and turned it off one more time, and walked into the kitchen to grab a beer from the fridge. With his eyes following my every move, I then sat down, next to him on the couch, and popped the top on that beer can as he yelled at me defiantly, with his fist in the air, screaming:

"NO!!!"

To which I replied with a scream of urgency and sarcasm,

"If it's good enough for you, then it's good enough for me!!"

The anger in my heart burst wide open at that moment, yet he did not care as he immediately started drinking again anyway, and I left. Not long after that, I ended up in the hospital with issues my doctor attributed to what was going on emotionally with both of my parents, and she recommended my mother and I seek counseling. I reluctantly went, but even the counselor said until one of us was willing to meet in the middle, counseling would not help us. Also at this time, my dad had gotten pulled over and arrested once again, and I was so fed up when my aunt called to tell me that he was in jail, I told her they better leave him there and that I did not care he was in soiled clothes! As far as I was concerned, it was time for him to face his consequences. His drinking and driving was affecting everything and my thought process was, "What if someone got hurt or killed, because it could be me on the road he meets one day, and what if there is an accident and someone dies?" I was adamant, which is quite ironic when looking back on my life now.

In his sentencing, the judge gave him two choices: jail time or extended rehab at the VA Medical Center in Murfreesboro, TN. His lawyer talked him into rehab, explaining this was the last chance he would be given, or he would go to prison. I was just a few weeks away from my eighteenth birthday, and it couldn't get there quick enough. Because the day I turned eighteen was the day I was planning to leave my mother's house, for good this time. I had been wanting to escape for over a year, but the threat of being turned over to child services, like my friend Jasmine had experienced, kept me under the same roof until she went to work that day. By the time she came home from work, I had left with no explanation and no note.

Again, I ran from her just as the little girl in the woods had done all those years ago.

Lucky for me, God was still watching out for me no matter how many times I ran. That year he had placed me in a youth group with a leader named Matt Willetts who did his very best to show me God's love with no strings attached. He did not always agree with what I was doing or my decisions, but he did let me talk and he did sit and listen, whenever the opportunity arose. He knew my intentions for coming to church were more about me getting away from home than being close to God, but it did not stop him from praying for me and telling me that I was loved. God had also placed in my path another couple who would provide me with stability. Stan and Cathy are still in my life today and although our relationship developed because of my friendship with their daughter, they became another set of parents to me. They offered to let me stay with them when I moved out that May afternoon, from my mother's house, knowing I needed a safe place to land, with all that had transpired. And in August, when it came time to go to college, they were the ones who drove me to MTSU in Murfreesboro, even on short notice, so I could be close to my dad.

Out of everyone throughout my life, they have become some of the closest people I would confide in, about things that were trusted to no one else. Repeatedly, they always offered love and truth, beyond anything else. I am thankful, even today, that God interjected that sense of family at a time when it was not recognizable to me.

CHAPTER 4

Responsibility
《 —∞— 》

RIVETED WITH AN EAGERNESS TO embrace a new era of life, on my own, the world seemed wide open. I was eighteen-years-old. An adult. At least by society's standards. Out of my mother's house and onto a life full of wondrous possibilities.

I had absolutely no clue what turning eighteen would mean for me. I watched as friends were given new cars for graduation and attended celebrations with their families. Witnessing how excited their parents were to prepare and send them off to college, or for some to join the military. Compared to what I was experiencing, a twinge of jealousy erupted within and I would surmise how my own life did not fit the happiness I was observing around me, as friends were released into their adulthood. It would make me reflect on all of the unfulfilled promises my daddy had made to me as a little girl, when we would talk of the future. Contemplating conversations with my father, the man who had instilled dreams into his little girl's heart, filled with possibility, I remembered his encouragement that I could accomplish whatever I set my heart and mind to.

My Gift to God

Accompanied by promises, that he would be right by my side to urge me on. But, here I was, my future before me, as an adult and he was not there, for any of it. It left me empty inside.

Instead, I was trying to escape the home of my mother as quickly as possible, as we could not even stand the sight of each other. My graduation gift was a packet of paperwork that included insurance papers for my father, and a newfound responsibility to take care of his finances and needs. My send off to college included a phone call from my mother the morning she had agreed to accompany me to MTSU, explaining that she had changed her mind. As I stood, with the phone in my hand, staring at it in disbelief in the middle of Stan and Cathy's living room, they scrambled to figure out a way to, once again, step in where I needed some parental assistance. Here I stood, now with the responsibility to take care of my dad, and to start college and I was a mess. I was finally out of my mother's house and, although I had been working since the age of fifteen and trying to take care of my own needs, I had absolutely no idea what I was doing.

This was also the first time my dad had been sober since I was ten-years-old. He had received a shot of reality, and I was receiving one as well, and neither one of us knew what to do. His motivation to get better, at this point, was that I was going to begin college. He was overjoyed when I arrived that day in Murfreesboro. True to his promises from those younger years, he stayed right by my side,

Responsibility

exuberantly helping me choose my major, register for classes, and purchasing supplies and books, because this was something he knew a lot about.

Prior to the stroke, he had just become a partner in his accounting firm, he was working on his doctorate, and was teaching classes at the local college. He knew what this world was like and he knew what success looked like. As a little girl, he had shown me what that looked like also. Always by his side, I would go to work with him and type on the typewriter while he worked, which I know sounds antiquated now. But, I loved it and wanted to be just like him, and now here we stood in the middle of this college campus, a sober father and a daughter, trying to find a new normal, once again.

I finally had his attention.

I had my independence from my mother, which I had wanted also. It seemed things were coming together, yet I had no idea how to handle all of the recent developments. Included in these recent changes was the beginning of a new relationship with a guy, named Dawson. He was a few years older and attempted to take care of me by filling in the gaps where he witnessed all of the missing pieces of my life. He was not new to responsibility, having lost his father a couple of years prior and was attempting to help guide me through all of this newfound independence and responsibility.

Still suppressing the desires that kept creeping up repeatedly, the next several years became a mixture of learning to care for my dad,

My Gift to God

how to be in a relationship with a man, although not married, and the beginning of a successful career path. All I really have to say about these years is that they taught me a lot about life. There was absolutely no pursuit on my part towards God and I rarely entered the doors of a church, or opened my bible, much less prayed. It was just not on my mind at all. There was no relevancy for me and although I was not against God, as far as I could see, I had nothing to gain or lose by being in church. After eight years, Dawson and I married and it was primarily to just finally do it after being together so long. There was no proposal. It was treated more like a business decision than a lifetime commitment with the person you loved. Now do not get me wrong, I did love Dawson, but not in the way a wife loves her husband and I knew the day we got married, even just moments prior to taking our vows, that I was about to go against God's plan.

The day of our wedding was not a romantic day. I wanted it to be the fairytale I had looked at in bridal magazines, but it was not. It probably appeared that way from the outside, but there was a lot lost in the details, such as the argument we got into that morning. The entire day just felt like it was something that needed to get checked off the list. Minutes before we were about to take our vows, standing on the platform before everyone, we were talking, or rather, he was complaining while I just looked at him, with a tedious smile on my face. Thinking to myself, aren't we supposed to be whispering sweet

Responsibility

nothings to each other while everyone was looking at us? Even though I had only been in church in recent years to pay the deposit for the one we were about to be married in, I knew in the depths of my heart, in those minutes prior to our vows being spoken, that I was making a mistake. I was choosing to get married for everyone else, and I wanted to turn and run out of that church. But, when I turned around and looked at a church full of guests, our families and our attendants, my feet felt like concrete. So, I turned back around, took a deep sigh of resoluteness, and prayed silently for God to help me, before vowing myself to this man that I knew I should not. But, I felt I had no other alternative. You know they say hindsight is twenty/twenty and well, it really is. We did not break up in the eight years prior to getting married, we did not have other relationships, but we separated for the first time one month after getting married, a second time within a couple of months later, and then my life took a dramatic turn.

I had become friends with a girl named Stacey, whom I had met through a close family friend. We began spending a great deal of time together and Dawson's job required that he travel extensively for work. One week, while he was out of town, I had become very ill with severe bronchitis and pneumonia and had been lying on my couch for days, attempting to recuperate. Stacey had come by to check on me several times to deliver food, Gatorade to stay hydrated, and movies to keep me occupied. I don't remember all of the details of that visit except for this; she had been there for some time and at one point while lying on the bed trying to get some rest after talking, she began caressing my hair to help me go to sleep. After lying on the bed beside me for several minutes, she leaned down and pressed her lips to mine softly, and kissed me. In that one minute, everything came to a halt and still frames exploded from within, of what had just happened.

In that one instant, my whole life pivoted.

Everything from that little six, seven, eight, and nine-year-old little girl, came rushing back.

Everything I had been suppressing, was no longer to be suppressed.

The desires of that little girl that had been prematurely activated, encompassed me fully and I thought:

"This is it. This is real. This is who I am."

One week later, after Dawson returned home, we separated again for the final time and I filed for divorce one month later. Our relationship had lasted eight years and our marriage barely made it six months, although the actual finalization of the divorce, took years. He was confused and I felt more alive than I had ever felt before.

Finally, something in my life made some kind of sense to me.

I knew that those feelings were real and no longer did I have to deny them, at least to Stacey I did not. No one else understood why I had left Dawson, and he did not know either. We were determined to stay in our own little happy world for as long as we could, because although we both felt exuberant, we did not expect our friends or family to understand, so we remained "in the closet" for quite a long time.

CHAPTER 5

Coming Out Alive
« —∞— »

STILL CARING FOR MY DAD, MY mother and I barely had any type of relationship to speak of, my divorce was taking forever to become final, and Stacey and I were now living together trying to keep everything a secret, because in those days being gay was not looked upon quite as favorably as it is today. She was facing her own demons from her childhood, and as a result of the stresses of trying to come to terms with everything, our relationship turned very tumultuous and abusive, quickly. I had never experienced the depths of abuse I was about to experience, and it was here that the devil really began playing tricks with me.

My mother and I had a very obstinate relationship, but she had never abused me physically.

My father was an alcoholic, and although he was not very present during my adolescence, he did not mentally, emotionally, and verbally abuse me the way Stacey began to torment me. And although my mother had problems talking to me, she never silenced me.

My Gift to God

I was entering into a time in my life where the devil so deceptively had a hold on me that although I was experiencing abuse from every angle, I would have told you I was more free than I had ever been in my life.

Stacey and I were together for five years, and in the beginning, I thought our relationship would continue until death do us part. Not all of the five years were bad and I do not want to paint a picture of it in that regard, but the reality of it, after the newness and the celebration of coming alive with my desires had worn off, it became disturbing. The interesting thing was that we related so much to each other on so many levels. She had gotten saved as a young girl, just as I had. We would go to church together, read the bible together, and even pray together. God was more present in that relationship than in the eight years prior with Dawson, so again I thought,

"Wow, this is great! I have had these feelings for girls growing up and I grew up in church and now the two can be joined together."

I thought that finally, we would be able to attend church together, no one had to know what we were doing at home, and we could just live our life.

And, to make sure we were not going against God, we prayed together, a very sincere prayer of, "God, take this from us if it is not of you, but if you do not, then we will know that it is okay."

Praying aloud with tears streaming down our cheeks, grasping fingers interlaced, the intensity of how deeply those confessing words meant to us was transforming to our relationship. What neither of us understood though, was that God was not in the taking business, rather He receives what we give. For the first time in my life, I felt I could honestly rely on someone else that not only knew, but also understood, what had been trapped inside of me all of these years and who also understood the feelings that had made me feel evil. We shared and talked about more than I had ever felt was allowed.

She got me.

She understood me.

She knew how to love me.

But at some point, being "in the closet" was too much to manage and we began revealing our relationship to select friends. Being inseparable resulted in our families taking notice, as well. Seeking out like-minded people and couples that understood us, we began searching out gay nightclubs discreetly. Sometimes in Chattanooga, sometimes we would drive to Nashville or Knoxville, just to be able to be us, out in public, so to speak, in the clubs.

It was here that the drinking began, because as they say, when in Rome, do as the Romans do. So, I did. I did not really enjoy it at first and would sometimes take on the role as the designated driver or make sure I had a pack of gum to kill the taste of the beer, but

My Gift to God

eventually I gave in to it as well. It became a normal occurrence on Fridays and Saturdays, to go home and relax a little after work, eat dinner so we didn't drink on an empty stomach, before arriving at the club a little before time for the drag show to start. We always wanted to ensure we could get a good seat, have time for a couple of shots, and maybe dance a little bit, prior to taking our seats for the main event. Then, after the show, dance and drink some more until it was time to make our way to the closest Waffle House where the waitress knew what I wanted when I walked in the door.

"Just give me a loaf of bread, I need to sober up!" with laughter permeating the drunken air.

How many times had I said growing up that I wanted to be just like my daddy? And here I was. Not an alcoholic, but drinking, it helped me to forget.

It helped me to forget that just under six months into this amazing relationship, where I was more alive than I had ever been allowed to be in my life, there were days I could not get out of bed because of the beating I had endured the night before. Somewhere between loving each other and reconciling ourselves and our relationship to God, the stress of hiding buckled us into one evening where I found myself hiding under a pool table, so she could not get to me. She eventually weeded me out with a baseball bat, though. I did not understand how she could be making passionate love to me one minute and beating me the next. Then in one fell swoop it would be like she woke up and would begin apologizing repeatedly about how sorry she was and promising that she would never do it again.

She would promise to never put bruises where anyone would be able to see them again.

She would promise to never make me cry again.

She would promise to love me and protect me.

And I would believe her.

The drinking also helped me forget an evening in Nashville at an isolated gay club, in a remote part of town. Upstairs, in the darkened balcony, she convinced me to have sex there. This resulted in a colossal verbal altercation that landed us in the parking lot, where I refused to get into the car with her. Running from the doors of that venue, she proceeded to chase me in the rain through darkened, drunken, middle of nowhere streets, surrounded by barbed wire fences and run down, empty manufacturing buildings. With nowhere to go and so far from home, I conceded after I retrieved my car keys, that she had thrown through a barbed wire fence. Soaked from the inside out, we finally went back to our cheap hotel room where all I desired was a warm shower to wash it all away. Instead, I found myself forced onto the bed, constrained to have sex with her repeatedly, until I hurt so bad that I bled from the incessant impact against me.

Now, please understand, I was not a victim in all of this, I was actually a willing participant. Knowing that statement is controversial, I will tell you I knew I could leave at any time. My problem was that I felt that I had absolutely nowhere to turn to. Because I had taken such an adamant stand for our relationship and for my lifestyle as a homosexual, I had to make this work. Determined for this relationship to endure and overcome in order for us to stay together for the rest of our lives, I sought every avenue possible to make the violence cease.

I tried to make the madness stop, by fighting her back.

By not fighting her back.

By yelling and screaming, and by being silent.

Nothing worked.

On the outside, to the friends and family who knew about us, our relationship appeared perfect. We had a beautiful home, my career was on the fast track, she was in college, and we were helping raise her niece, nephew, and one of her younger cousins. We were also in discussion with her aunt and uncle about her cousin moving in with us and becoming a part of our household. We became adept at the deception that outwardly our relationship was more perfect than anyone else's and that we were able to handle anything that came our way together. The deception was so thoroughly received that other people would even come to us for advice or assistance in relationship and other matters. We both became masters at this, without one single discussion that that was what we were doing. But, when no one was around, our relationship mounded up to a pile of ashes. All the outward façade we would put on for everyone else would disappear, and we were left with just each other.

We had both reconciled our feelings to God's plan and determined that we were meant to be together because God had not answered our prayers that if this was not of Him, for Him to take it from us. So in our minds and hearts it became right and nothing to be concerned about as far as how our eternity would be affected. As the years progressed we began taking a stand and "coming out of the closet" with the majority of our friends and family that did not already have knowledge of our relationship, so that we no longer had to hide it. This was an attempt to constitute a more bearable relationship, or at least it seemed that way.

This in itself was its own form of deception by the devil, because the more we came out of the closet, the more I was able to make a stand that I was gay and if you don't like it, you don't have to be around me. My thought process at the time was that: I have my friends, I have my chosen family, and that is all that I need.

Coming out of the closet to my mother was quite the event. I knew she was aware I was in a relationship with Stacey because she had asked me early on in our friendship,

"How good of friends are you and Stacey?" and my response was,

My Gift to God

"Don't ask a question, that you don't want the truth to. But if you want me to tell you the truth, I will." That is precisely where that conversation ended.

Fast forward two years later, I prepared an elaborate dinner for her, Stacey and I, and Stacey's step-mother, who was accepting of us. I had formulated this majestic event, with a table full of homemade food I spent all day cooking, laid out in our formal dining room, using the fine china. I was nervous about actually speaking the words to her, but was anticipating the look in her eyes when I spoke the words to her face. I wanted the reaction! I had taken a Xanax to relax, which was not customary for me to take any medication, and then my mother arrived. We ate, and I proceeded to commence into this elaborate speech to which my mother wanted no part of. When I finally spoke the words and the tears started streaming down her face as she told me I was going to hell, it afforded me the opportunity to reject my mother, right before she rejected me. I demanded that she either accept us as a couple or have no relationship with us, or me, whatsoever.

Because my mother called our relationship a "situation" that evening, I refused any contact with her for over two years. Denying her any access to me at all, she would send letters and I would have them returned, unopened. I blocked her number from receiving phone calls and when she sent letters to my grandmother for me, I would instruct her to send them back. My Mammaw tried her best to get me to acknowledge my mother in some way, but I refused adamantly that she have any thread of anything that related to me. Looking back, I see the isolation that the devil was creating and that I was allowing him to create. Although I was still caring for my father, in some ways, I was keeping him at arms-length as well. I had moved him into an apartment so that we could both maintain some sense of independence, even though he no longer drove a vehicle. I would take him groceries when he needed them, clean his house, and spend some time with him, but his days became filled with studying, watching television, and being interested in my career and success. Those were the main points our conversations became focused on. Well, that and football, as we both loved to watch college ballgames.

So, my relationship with my father was okay, with my mother non-existent, with God as long as he was not judging me, and only with friends and family that accepted Stacey and I together. The more the isolation encroached on my life, silently, so did the coexistence of our lives becoming inseparable. Slowly, a progression began that she had to be with me wherever I went. She had to go to work with me, to the grocery store with me, to my dad's with me, to my Mammaw's, to take a shower, to go to friends. I could not talk on the phone or be involved in a conversation with anyone, unless she was present.

Anywhere. It was together. Or it was nowhere.

My Gift to God

This is when the mental and verbal abuse began. When I purchased clothes, she wanted us to have matching articles, identical, maybe a slightly different color scheme, but the same clothes and shoes. I would go to have my hair cut and Jody, who was my hairdresser and friend, was the first person to ask me why I did not get the style I wanted instead of what Stacey was telling me to get. I started saying because she knows what looks good on me. It was better to go along with her than endure the wrath of when we left. Because every time we left somewhere, whether a friend's house, getting my hair done, getting off the phone, or buying clothes, I was questioned extensively.

Why did you do this?

Why did you do that?

Why did you say this or that?

You should be funnier or you should not talk as much.

You should have said this, not that.

Why did you look at her like that?

What did this mean when you did this?

Don't do that.

You make me look like a fool, or even better than that, you made yourself look stupid.

In essence, I became no one.

My voice became silent. I turned into just the girl with Stacey, who is really smart in business with a good career, but otherwise she is pretty boring. She's pretty, but she never says a word. It was funny after Stacey and I broke up, there were many friends that we had acquired mutually over the years as a couple, who all had the same response:

"You do have a voice? Man, you never talked, why were you so quiet?"

None of them knew the dissertation I would have to give after them leaving or on our way home from being with other people. So I chose to become silent. It was easier that way. Because if not, what I received alone, became too great. One such evening, when we still lived in a downstairs apartment, we had come home from being with friends. She was questioning me, as was normal, and we pulled into the parking lot into a space next to the cop who lived upstairs from us with his wife, who was getting out of his patrol car. We nodded to each other and went into each of our separate apartments. As we entered our apartment, Stacey was barraging me with questions and becoming increasingly antagonistic. I was unable to derive whatever answer she was probing me for incessantly about why I had behaved in a particular manner while at our friend's home. Unable to solve the mystery and deliver the presumed answer, the further the level of her anger and cursing was amplified until finally she pushed me to the floor, dragged me by my feet into the living room, while I clawed at the walls with my fingers. She proceeded to position herself on top of me with my arms and legs restrained under her, while she launched into a tirade beating my head into the thin carpet against the hard concrete floor.

I could not escape her. While lying there rummaging the depths of my diaphragm in an attempt to produce a piercing scream for help, she held me down, laughing at me, telling me how weak I was, and that there was no one that would dare help me. I screamed at the top of my lungs, hoping the cop upstairs would come to my rescue, but he never did. He wanted no involvement with a domestic dispute between two women. Walking above us, I could hear his footsteps pacing the floor, but the shrill echoing from my vocal chords merely produced riotous laughter from Stacey, with her head lunging back in enjoyment at my discomfort. I screamed until the noise exiting my throat became torturous. Eventually, I stopped screaming for help and launched into begging for her to kill me as my entire body began resonating pain. Although soft in tone, the connotation of words was genuine as I commanded her to get it over with, while informing her I believed that one day she would kill me, whether she meant to or not. The amusement for her persisted until boredom from the game overtook her. With one final punch to my torso and an expression of disgust thrown my way, she jumped off of me. Grabbing the keys to my car, she left me laying on the floor of that apartment, alone, in pain, and went to find some weed to smoke. At that time, the abuse was kept internally, but nearing our fifth year anniversary, these confrontations were spiraling out of control.

The abuse was becoming more noticeable, and the mental games she played started surfacing in front of our friends. I still felt isolated and unable to leave until one day I came home from work, pulled into the driveway, and walked inside where she had been laying on the couch all day, lazily. She was expecting me to fix her dinner, to which I informed her I was not going to. Her attention sparked to this unusual behavior. She arose swiftly and chased me back outside and in the middle of the day she jumped me in the driveway and began beating my head against the asphalt. Staring at her in disbelief that she would allow the neighbors the opportunity to witness this, I very quietly, with hot steamy tears pouring down my cheeks, spoke against her rage that day. Articulating to her ears deliberate lingering words, "Today is the day. You kill me today or you get off of me, because this is the last time you will beat me. This is the last opportunity for you to try and destroy me."

She continued until no longer she got what she was looking for. I felt completely dead inside, as I felt the warm blood seeping down the back of my head, matting up my hair interlaced with bits of asphalt. I walked quietly to our bedroom, in the back of the house, packed a small bag that I found in the closet, and walked briskly back down the hallway, into the living room. She had taken up residence, once again, on the couch watching television. As she tried to ignore me, I informed her I was leaving for three days, and when I returned I expected her to be gone from my house. With her usual laughter, she did not take me seriously, but never had I been more profoundly resolute than I was in that very moment.

I told her, "Take what you want, but you cannot have me any longer."

She thought I was joking, and it took longer than three days for her to leave and although she did take everything she possibly could, it did not matter what physical possessions she extracted. Because, I knew, that was the last day I would ever accept a beating from anyone.

No longer would I have to hide at night and sleep in my office at work, where she had no key to get in or access to me.

No more would I have to answer as to why I did or said something.

No longer would I have to put up with her mind games or playing the game of apparent perfection while I waited on the anger to rage against me at home, when we were alone.

Finally, I would no longer be silenced.

I would not have to attend another high school reunion, after fighting in the parking lot, because I was embarrassed that we were dressed identically, but she would not let me go in alone.

No longer would I have to contend with wearing long sleeves to hide the bruises or pretend that I was cramping because the wounds on my torso were excruciating.

But now, I had to find my identity again and I realized that I had pushed so many people away. Where did I have to turn to?

I did not want to admit that our relationship was a failure. I did not want to face the questions, or the accusations of the stand I had taken as Stacey's wife and life partner. Realizing that I would lose some valuable relationships with her family and a few friends was a difficult decision. Because I knew that ending the relationship with her meant that I had to cut certain ties in order to avoid contact with her. And by doing that, when I took stock of who was left, there were not many people, especially family. My Aunt Vonda and Uncle Randy had remained steadfast as a positive and safe influence over the course of those five years, even though they did not approve of our lifestyle. But, even with them, I had to distance myself, slightly, because Stacey continued to arrive unannounced at their home, expecting to find me there.

My mother and I had actually resumed speaking after the two years of isolation, but I knew I could not call upon her without looking into her eyes and seeing a look of satisfaction that this relationship was finally over.

Our silence had come to an end after she called, from an unrecognizable number, hesitantly, on a Mother's Day over two years after that planned dinner, where I had come out to her in arrogance. And when I heard her voice for the first time, my heart broke wide open realizing that I had, in fact, missed her. That conversation did not fix everything, but it was a beginning. I continued to defy her at any given moment as she remained unrelenting at her interjection of disapproval. Persistently, she would convey that she was praying for me and I would vehemently scrutinize her exclaiming,

"What are you praying for? Because if you are not praying what I want you to pray, then I don't want your prayers for me!"

Adamantly, I would challenge her still, but I thank God today that she never stopped praying. She never gave up hope that one day we would be reconciled. At one point of desperation she even dedicated me back to God and told Him that she knew He had given her the gift of a daughter that she had always longed for. But she also knew that He loved me even more than she did. So she would pray for my protection morning, noon, and night. Without ceasing, no matter how many times or how adamantly I challenged her. I know today that the prayers of a mother's heart for her child are like no other prayers! She loved me enough to give me back to the one who created me in her very womb.

However, our relationship continued on the treacherous slope it had been on for so many years, with no real stability, even after she called me. We were reconciled to the fact that I was her daughter and she was my mother, but that was about it, at least on my part. We continued an arm's length relationship for well into another decade. For although my relationship with Stacey was coming to an end, my relationship with women was continuing, and I knew she did not approve.

CHAPTER 6

Regaining Freedom
« —∞— »

AFTER STRUGGLING TO MANAGE the arduous exit of Stacey from my life, and the laborious reality of making her realize I was never entertaining the thought of entering back into a relationship with her, again I felt some freedom. This had been a very long and difficult five years for me. A few months later, I began dating another girl, who I had met briefly through friends, about a year earlier. She had captivated my attention and although there had been a yearning to learn more about her, the suffocating supervision of Stacey had left no room for even a slightly intriguing conversation between the two of us, even as friends. So, imagine her surprise when I contacted her via email to initiate at least the possibility of a friendship.

I learned she had moved to New York City, and with copious amounts of dialogue it was evident we desired to learn more about each other. On a brisk, fall evening, several months following our first reunited contact, she flew back to Tennessee. Once I anxiously picked her up from the airport, we drove to the same house where I had originally met her, to surprise our friends who were gathered around a beautiful bonfire. They had no idea she was arriving with me and I was not prepared that she would not only captivate my attention, once again, but, also, my heart that weekend. Subsequently, I traveled to New York City to visit her and it was not long after that memorable trip, that one evening, I drove thirteen hours in order to move her back to Tennessee. We dated for a few years and I can say unequivocally that our love was a deeper, more passionate love than I had experienced up to that point in my life. There was only one problem, and it had manifested into a greater hindrance than I recognized. My identity had slowly been stripped away in the previous five years, and it still tarnished me. I did not really know who I was, outside of work, because that had been the only avenue that involved me and my own accomplishments and had not revolved around my relationship with Stacey. Outside of my career, I had become a follower. This was challenging with Adriana because she was attracted to my independence, not the girl who suddenly wanted to be involved with whatever interested her.

And I had no idea how to do that anymore, because my own interests had, literally, been beaten out of me.

I was slowly learning how to become my own person again, but our relationship eventually ended due in a large part to this. It was around this time the pendulum swing happened, where it was no longer about what everyone else wanted, and it became all about me.

Regaining Freedom

I jokingly call this the Sarah century because now I was not only going to not allow anyone to beat or abuse me, but I was determined to not let anyone close enough to hurt me, in any manner. Physically and emotionally, I began erecting a ginormous protective structure surrounding every area of my life that could not be infiltrated. I changed courses dutifully, asking myself each and every day,

What do I want to do today?

What do I want out of life?

What is going to make me happy, today?

I could care less about anyone else's feelings because that had proved to be futile, and I wanted no part of it. I determined that, as long as I was good and happy, that is all that mattered from here forward. Applying that mantra daily, is precisely how I began approaching my life and my future.

During this time not only was I drinking, but I began experimenting with drugs and adventure. My happiness incorporated whatever high I chose at the moment. Smoking pot on a regular basis allowed a very mellow, happy escape where there was no concern with becoming too intoxicated and feeling putrid. At this point, that type of escape held no allure for me and I sought adventurous alternatives such as mushrooms, acid, and cocaine. I was also spending all of my free time and weekends on the Ocoee River, whitewater rafting, and hanging out at the outpost with all of the other guides. It was easy for me to escape there. I found whatever I wanted to entertain and enjoy myself with a completely stress free, relaxed crowd, a close knit group of friends.

There was no pretense with this group. You did not have to try and be anybody but yourself and that appealed to me greatly. It fulfilled my search for myself and the things I, alone, loved without the influence of someone else dictating my preferences. Each day became a new day and an easy search for happiness. This was the first of several summers I spent with these friends, and I looked forward each winter to being reunited with them in the spring. I was still dating women, at the time, and became the token lesbian at the river, which was cool with me. It was easy for me and I had no expectations from anyone I had to live up to.

Somewhere in the midst of this all, I suddenly had this newfound feeling that I was invincible. I had established control of my happiness and had set the parameters with which I would allow anyone to come into my life. Thus, it was easy for me to think I had gained some strength in my own safety or protection.

Guarding my heart, I closed it off and learned to show those I wanted to be involved with just enough affection to want to be with me, but not enough that they could break the barriers I was continuing to erect.

If I thought there was a chance of someone getting through and close enough to me to bring about any type of emotion, specifically if someone had the power to make me cry, I eliminated them immediately from my life. With absolutely no explanation and delivering no answers to their questions of why.

My protection from hurt and my lust for happiness and pleasure was all I was concerned with. I hurt person after person with no regard for their feelings and emotions. It did not matter to me, in the least, if they were hurt due to my disregard as long as it had no lasting effect on me. The coldness and hardness did not even feel real, because each day I was doing whatever the heck I wanted to do that particular day, so it all just slid right off of my back easily.

My search for this happiness, however, was missing one key element, an eternal happiness. Everything was temporary, which meant I had no investment in it, but neither did I have an investment in my relationship with God.

I was just doing as I pleased, but God was still reaching through the haze, from time to time, to capture my attention.

The first of many of these was through a guy, named Adam. I had met him while still dating Adriana, and we had become friends. We started spending quite a bit of time together, after my relationship with her ended, and we just got along pretty easily, which was right up my alley. But one night, things changed. It was getting close to my birthday and he had asked if I wanted to come out to his property for dinner. I replied, "Sure, why not?"

When I arrived, however, I knew, instantly, this was no regular visit, but a date.

My Gift to God

Adam answered the door wearing his Scottish Kilt and native attire and had spent all afternoon in preparation for this dinner. Entering the hallway, he led me discreetly to the dining room to a table that was set complete with flowers and a wonderful dinner. He had also baked homemade scones for my birthday, which he knew to be my favorite. After dinner, he explained that he needed to change clothes because he had another surprise awaiting us. He knew I loved to shoot guns and that my daddy had taught me how to shoot several years prior to his stroke. He also understood it was not something I had much opportunity to do any longer. So, he had set up half a dozen targets, around the property, with different guns, and he walked me out in the field to lead me to the first target.

There was nothing more perfect to me, than that moment.

One particular target was an orange about 100 yards away. For this meticulous object he had set me up with a rifle, which I had never shot before. So, here I was lying in a field, with a skirt on, aiming at an orange through iron sights, and I blew the peel off that orange but left the inside of it sitting where it had started, intact. It was awesome!!! I could probably never make that shot again, but with his instruction to sight it in, take a deep breath, let my breath out real slow, and then smoothly pull the trigger, it happened. I was ecstatic!

Once target practice was completed, we walked back to the house and as we sat on the front porch, he explained he had something to give me. He then proceeded to hand me a necklace, a set of two strands of pearls that he had hand strung, himself, and a 9mm Beretta, as a birthday present.

Shocked and in sheer disbelief, I knew, I was in trouble.

This guy knew me!

And not only did he know me, he understood that I had this tomboyish side to me, but also this girlie girl side that most people did not get.

He was courting me, and I had no idea what to do with that.

CHAPTER 7

God Speaks
《 —∞— 》

SOMETHING ELSE HAPPENED THAT night out at Adam's. After target practice and after he presented me with those magnificent gifts, we walked back out in the field with a bottle of wine and a blanket and we became intimate for the first and only time in that decade. But the something else that happened, it was not the intimacy, it was God. He spoke directly to my heart, for the second time in my life. But, what God told me, that star filled evening, threw me into utter confusion.

As the moon began rising in the beautiful, crisp, clear evening, He told me that this man, Adam, was my husband. I remember looking at Adam in the moonlight, after this moment of intimacy, and thinking,

"Oh, My, Gosh! How am I going to get out of this one?!"

I began that night and the next morning to argue with God.

I told God:

"Hold up, you know who I am!

My Gift to God

We have already been through all of this back when I was dating Stacey.

Remember, God, I'm gay, remember that?!

You did not take it from me and even though now I have had sex with Adam that does not make him my husband, and it certainly does not make me straight. That was just a thing.

Come on now, God, get with the program and quit jacking me around like this!"

But, it was clear to me that I had, in fact, heard God say that to me. The next day when Adam came by my house, I dropped him like a hot potato. Not just because I was so confused as to what I had heard God say to me, but also because I knew, if what I heard was true from God, that I would not and could not defile Adam. I could not afford to make him another one of my pawns in my game of happiness. I also knew and respected Adam enough to know that I would destroy him in my relentless pursuit of happiness that included adventures he was not involved in. Adam did not understand and we did not have a break up conversation or anything like that. I just cut him off from having any real closeness with me that could potentially lead to anything else happening. I still had the gun and the pearls, but I did not want to be the keeper of his heart. I did not want that responsibility. We remained friends and would continue to see or talk to each other here and there, but with no physicality whatsoever.

God Speaks

But God was not finished with my one-sided conversation where I attempted to shut him down.

Instead, He started interjecting into my life moments I would not be able to deny that it was Him. I would choose to just shrug them off, but He kept after me, time and time again. One such instance, I was at one of the river hangouts called The Duff, which was a popular river bar for all of the guides and local hippies. I had arrived with a friend of mine and, after several drinks, had gone outside for something and there was an older gentleman in the parking lot.

He walked over and started talking to me, attempting to convince me that he knew who I was. Not recognizing this man, he then asked where my husband, Adam, was. I looked at him, confused, this really clean cut, completely sober, gray haired man, dressed in a polo shirt and slacks, who did not fit in at all with the surroundings, and I asked him with a quizzical voice and facial expression,

"You mean, Laxton!?" because the guy I was with at the bar, his first name was Adam, but I always called him Laxton instead of Adam. The man replied emphatically.

"No. Adam. Where is your husband, Adam?"

I proceeded to inform him he had no idea what he was talking about, that I was not married, had no plans of being married, and he must be confused. He then began telling me things about my life and bringing up people from my past that no stranger, much less most people in my life, had any knowledge of whatsoever. I began to think to myself, "Those drinks The Duff is serving up tonight must be some really good stuff." However, I was not very intoxicated when this conversation took place and when I finally decided to walk away, and turned around to say one last thing to him, he was gone.

God's footprint remained, though, and I took note of it in my heart.

Not only were these things happening individually, but on the rare occasions that Adam and I would still see each other, random people would call us husband and wife or prophesy that we were going to be married. Neither of us can tell you how many times that happened, even to this day, but it became almost comical that we could not spend any time together at all without it occurring. God was trying to open my eyes and my heart, but I was refusing to see it or to listen. I knew that Adam cared for me and was becoming increasingly frustrated with my disengagement, but in my heart, I was still gay. Besides taking note of all that was happening, I chose to not let it have a lasting hold until nearly a decade later.

So, I ran again, just this time, it was from what I considered to be nonsense.

Ignoring the gibberish, I carried on with my life and its happiness mantra, pursuing only those things that benefited me in my career and personal pursuits. During this time, I was dating several different women and was so arrogant that I hosted a Christmas party, at my house one year, and invited every single one of them, along with all of my friends. With no regard for each of their feelings, I watched them all collide into the realization of what I was doing, and that it did not matter to me. I took the stance that, if they wanted to be around me, I was not going to hide anything from any of them. I was so bold and brazen to think my honesty held some type of honor because I was being open and honest about it all.

Looking back, I see the coldness with which the devil was beginning to encapsulate my heart and the truth that my honesty held no real integrity, at all.

It was all about me.

I began courting different women and would leave a date with one to go and meet another. Hardly ever home, if I took a whim to jump on a plane and go to Salt Lake City or Dallas, or anywhere else, I would do it. If someone wanted to go with me, they could. If not, I was fine to go by myself. I was sure to meet some new friends wherever I went. My voice was definitely no longer stifled, just my heart. My family was my family. I saw them when I wanted to, but only just enough to stay in contact. My dad was doing well, and as far as I knew, my mother was good, although I knew no details of what was going on in her life.

My closest family member was my Mammaw, who, throughout all of these years and conflict, had been the only true, steady force that kept me connected with the rest of my family. I visited her often and would get angry when she would tell me that, both, Adam and

My Gift to God

Stacey had been by to see her multiple times. She knew, more than anything, it was in hopes they would find me there, or to find out what I was up to.

But, it was fine, because my Mammaw was easy to love and she knew, more than anyone I had ever known, how to truly love others.

CHAPTER 8

My Mammaw

« —∞— »

MY MATERNAL GRANDMOTHER continually influenced my life, as few other family members had the opportunity to. Throughout childhood, teenage, and my adult years her influence remained steady, consistent, and trustworthy. Even though she called and told me I was going to hell after learning of my involvement with Stacey, from my mother, she called back within minutes of that conversation and apologized. She did not recant what she had said, but her apology was, that no matter what, she loved me and that what she was concerned with was my eternity. She did not understand, and did not really care to understand. However, she was determined to love me and whomever I loved, first and foremost. Mammaw allowed no isolation from her firstborn grandchild. Although her heart hurt for the tainted relationship that my mother and I had, she knew it went deeper than just the admonition that I was gay. She had lived with my mother and I shortly after my dad's stroke and bore witness to the many fights and tensions that were present in that relationship.

My Gift to God

Attempting to become a voice of reason and a protector from the pain and confusion, she strove to provide a place of comfort and truth.

Endeavoring to establish my independence, there was an instance when I was eleven, that she provided that sense of security, protection, and voice of reason for me. At a local state park that honored the local Indian heritage, a Girl Scout's retreat was being held that included a day full of activities, with the option of overnight camping. This was a significant event with numerous other troops, from the surrounding area, also involved, in order that we may earn badges while allowing us to interact with each other. My mother had merely authorized me to spend the day there, instead of staying for the evening bonfire and camping. At the end of the afternoon, I was to take the bus, back to the mall in town. My Mammaw was scheduled to pick me up there, since my mother would be at work. However, I was having so much fun with all of the crafts, workshops, and learning about the Native American culture that I did not want to leave.

Exuberantly, I witnessed the girls set up their campsites and the adults prepare for the massive bonfire that was to take place after dark. A Cherokee Indian dance production was also planned to take place, after dinner, in the outdoor pavilion. There was going to be fire twirling, roasting marshmallows and all sorts of things that reminded me so much of what my dad and I used to do on the weekends. I wanted to be a part of that so much! My heart longed for those moments outside under the stars, listening to the crackle of the fire, and laughter that would encircle it. When it came time for those of us who were not camping to load up on the school bus to return back to town, I made my own decision for that evening.

Ambling up the hill where the bus was waiting, I stood there, watching those climbing the steps of the bus and walking down the aisle to take their seats. Then I glanced down the hill, to my right, where I could see the adults setting up the bonfire, and the Cherokee Indians caught my eye. Observing their beautiful, ornate costumes, feathers, headdresses, and attire, preparing for the dance, I began to envision the wonderment of their dancing later in the evening. The smell of the evening meal wafted up through the air, joined with laughter from hundreds of little girls and, in that moment, I told myself, "Well, there is no one here to make me get on the bus and this is where I want to be." My troop leader had already told me she wanted me to stay and that they had enough stuff for me to camp with. So, I made the most rational decision that an eleven-year-old could make, I walked back down the hill, and joined my friends.

I did not realize that panic would arise once my Mammaw stopped by my mom's work to tell her I had not been on the bus when it arrived.

My mother thought I was missing and after calling some friends to help look for me, they drove out to the state park. One of the

My Gift to God

troop leaders found me and took me to the park lodge where my mother waited, both furious with me, but also excited that I had been found. I thought it was ridiculous. Where else would I be? Logically, I thought it would be pretty easy to figure out my location when I was not on the bus and they would know I just wanted to stay and everything would be alright. Funny, the logic of an eleven-year-old. I felt that my mother was dramatically seizing the opportunity to overreact by formulating that I was missing and needed locating. After many tears and her expressing her unhappiness at my independence and thoughtlessness, she did let me stay. But, when I returned home the next day, boy, did I pay for it.

A whipping with the belt and a yelling ensued that made no sense to me, since I had been allowed to stay. When she locked me in my room, I simply sat there in confusion. After my mother went to bed, my Mammaw came into my bedroom. In her slow, calm, sweet voice, she comforted me and just talked to me about how, maybe, I should have handled the situation differently. All the while, she cradled and loved me. She understood I missed the things I did with my dad before the stroke and that's why I wanted to stay for the camping. She also understood the longing had overpowered the concern. She told me she did not panic and figured that's where I was, but also, that I needed to understand where my mom was coming from, as well.

She knew me, and she definitely understood how to calm me.

My Mammaw

Even during the years I was not attending church, when I visited her, there was always the Gaither's or some other gospel group on the radio, or stereo playing in the background. She would relay what was going on at her church, and with the family, as that was really what her life revolved around. She invited me to attend church with her although not pressuring me or using the guilt card. More than anything she just wanted to know how I was, all the while just loving me. She did the same thing when she knew things were not right between Stacey and me, although I dared not say a word or let on that there was anything abusive taking place. She knew, sometimes, I just needed my Mammaw's hug no matter what was going on. So imagine my surprise when she called me one day and said, "We need to talk. Can you come over?" I went and picked her up so that we could go to Cracker Barrel to eat. She sat very quietly, simply pushing food around on her plate, and I knew something was up.

She began hem hawing around a little bit before finally raising her dainty, tear filled eyes to mine as she delivered the words. The doctor had told her she had cancer. She explained about a sore she had for some time, under one of her breasts, but she had not thought very much about it, until it would not heal. Once it started oozing, she decided to have it checked. This lady, my Mammaw, who had always been my protector, sat quietly across from me, with tears starting to slowly fall down her pretty cheeks. In that instant, the room and the people in it disappeared for me, and all I wanted were the answers.

Okay. Cancer.

What kind?

What do we do?

How do we fix it?

There has to be a way!

One week later, we found out it was stage four breast cancer and a decision on what to do, as far as treatment and chemotherapy, had to be made. We knew the chemotherapy would not cure it, but there was a possibility it may stop it from growing and, give us more time. She decided, after much contemplation, to try, even though she might lose her pretty, wavy, dark hair and would become weak and sick. She decided to try, for us, for her family, the unselfish person that she was. Her first appointment was scheduled and one morning she confided how scared she was, yet, she did not want anyone else to know. She also wanted to know, if I could be one of the family to accompany her to the treatments.

To this day, I cannot make the image of that cold chemotherapy room disappear from my mind.

The slow drops, dripping into her veins.

The eyes full of questions and fear that looked back at me as we sat and did puzzle books and watched daytime television, with blankets around our legs and a toboggan on her head.

My Mammaw

We laughed at the silly hats people made for the chemo room, trying to keep an affectionate spirit in the air and, she would sit and pat my hand, as she always liked to do, and call me Sarah Jane or Sarah Lee.

Some days, our conversations turned to questions during treatment and, others we could laugh and be silly, but no matter the spirit in the air was always that word, cancer, that lingered close by.

When we went back to her Oncologist, after the rounds of chemotherapy, to get the results of the latest PET scan, my Mammaw did not want to be in the room to hear the results. She knew the sore under her breast was not getting better, she felt weak, and was watching her black hair turn grey, as it thinned from the treatments. My aunt and I got the results, then my Mammaw wanted to talk with the doctor, alone.

Sitting in that hallway seemed like an entire day until the door opened. My little Mammaw, had made her decision.

Quality, versus quantity.

That had been one of our more sobering conversations in the chemo room. It was true, we wanted her to not be sicker than she had to be, or to suffer from something more than she already was. But, more sobering than hearing her decision to not pursue treatment, was hearing the words, six to nine months. How, we longed, for those words not to be true!

My Gift to God

Then came much planning. Where would she move to? Who would be responsible for this thing or that thing? Until, she adamantly put a halt to all of those conversations. It did not matter that I had taken a new, lucrative position that required travel. I planned to lay it aside so she could move in with me. I could care for her and try to protect her, as she had been my protector for so long. It did not matter that my Aunt Carla wanted her to move in with her, because they had enough room and privacy. Mammaw wanted to stay, with her cat, Missy, in her little apartment, just over the hill from my house, for as long, as possible.

And, that was final. She would not hear of me quitting my job or my aunt rearranging her house.

At least not yet, she wouldn't.

Mammaw wanted her life to be as normal as possible, for as long as possible, and she asked that we respect that. With daily visits, when I was in town, or daily phone calls when traveling, we kept in check with each other. Close to a month after that visit to the Oncologist, she told me she was starting to feel weak, but, again, she did not want her children to know. I explained what a predicament she was putting me in. She told me she knew she could tell me things, she could not tell the others because I could handle it, and not get overly emotional about it. So, at that moment, sitting in her living room, we made a pact with each other. I would keep her confidence, up until the point I knew something had to be done. I

My Mammaw

promised to not betray her confidence, as long as she trusted me to make that call. We both cried, she cradled me in her lap as she always liked to do (some things you just never get too old for), and then we talked about life and love. Adam and Stacey were still coming to visit and she asked if I minded. I told her it was fine. No matter the intentions, I knew they had come to love her, also.

She was one of the easiest people to love that I have ever known, and one of those people who could love without boundaries, no matter what had happened in the past. I wish I understood how to love that way!

Just over a month after our pact, she called and asked I come over earlier than usual. So, I headed on over and when I arrived, she was rocking in her recliner. I could sense she was nervous, with that rocker moving ninety to nothing, and I asked, "What's up, Mammaw?" She informed me she had fallen earlier in the day, and I said, "Okay, are you alright? What happened?" She then revealed, over the past couple of days, she had experienced a difficult time walking from the bathroom to the living room, and that she felt weaker than normal. Slowly, I sat down and said to her, "I think it's time, Mammaw. What do you want to do?"

Crying, she sat, rocking in her recliner, with me at her feet, holding her hand, silent for the longest time. Finally, she said, "I think I want to go to Carla's because it will be easier on everyone else. But, I have, so much, stuff!" Man, how we laughed and cried that day! We laughed about all of the stuff she had accumulated over her life, and what to do with it, and we cried about having to pack it all up. But, more than that, realization was setting in.

She wanted me to take her car I had bought her as a Christmas present, several years earlier, to my house because she was afraid to drive, and did not want the temptation. She did not want to hurt anyone, or hurt herself. The family planned to move her, but she insisted on being able to sort through her own belongings, give away or box up particular items, and also return gifts that had been given to her, over the years, to the people that had given them to her. In fact, she had already began dividing some things up, and the days quickly moved into packing and getting Carla's house ready in preparation for moving day.

During all of this, she maintained a grace of laughter and love, just as she had always done, and refused an air of sadness to surround us.

Moving day proved to be a pivotal moment for both of us. I arrived early in the morning and a couple of other family members were there, as well. She was still sitting in that recliner (it would be the last thing to go), giving instructions of what was going with her and what was being given away. She started telling me the washer and dryer was going to be given to Adam. He was apparently moving into a new apartment and she wanted to give him a few things. About ten minutes later, she stated she was also giving him the kitchen table and some pots and pans, among other items. After about the third time of her listing all the stuff she was giving to Adam, I looked at her and pronounced, self-righteously:

"Well, why don't you just give everything to him then? Why are we packing all of this stuff up?!"

She laughed at me as she pulled herself forward, slowly, in her recliner and said, "Hold on a second.... That, boy, affects you!"

To which I replied, "No, he doesn't! You have no idea what you are talking about!"

But, boy, did she know what she was talking about!

She told me that day, as she leaned back into her chair, "You just wait, Sarah, and you will see."

She then sent me on an errand to give some stuff away to some new neighbors. They did not have much and I welcomed the escape, especially when I came waltzing out the door to find Adam and my cousin with a trailer, ready to load things up. She had failed to mention he was coming that day. But then, who was I that she needed to tell? He and I did not speak very much that morning because I was so tore up and mad about what she had said. I was determined to prove to her, that he had absolutely no effect on me, at all.

It had to be quite hysterical from her perspective, sitting in that recliner, watching me prance around like nothing was wrong, all the while being sure to ignore him. She watched him, watch me, while he wondered what he had done to make me act that way. Oh, the joys of learning life. Every once in a while, she would laugh and cut a joke at me, just to get another rise, just because she could. So, moving day really was not that bad for everyone. She always set the stage for humor and laughter, even if that day, it was at my expense.

Getting settled at my Aunt Carla's was not very hard for Mammaw. She had Mammaw Wright, (my Aunt Carla's widowed mother-in-law), there for companionship and, they had always gotten along great. The house became a revolving door of visitors, which they were accustomed to, with all of their grandkids in and out. My daily visits went from over the hill, to driving thirty miles down the interstate, but it did not matter to me. At first, things were pretty normal, but a couple of weeks after moving, it became clear it was time to call hospice. Her health was not declining too fast yet, but the time was coming.

That was another heart wrenching day; meeting nurses and the hospice chaplain, watching them wheel in equipment, "just in case," and bring in prescriptions, "just in case," they were needed. What really rolled into the house that day, was another dose of realization. All of my aunts, and my mom, were there also and not one of us was prepared for what all of this meant. Even my mother, a nurse and my Aunt Vonda, a hospice nurse, were not prepared for this to be so close to home.

My Mammaw

Over the next three months, my Aunt Carla's home became a hotel, of sorts. My employer had allowed me to travel less and since I worked from a home office, with a laptop, I just changed the location from my house to theirs. I would leave occasionally to make the trip up the highway to wash clothes, take care of personal business and make sure my dad had groceries and was cared for. My two other aunts were in and out, daily as well, and my mother was down every day she had off, even though she was also caring for my stepdad, who had lung cancer. All of us combined, with Steve and Carla's kids and grandkids, coming and going, the door never needed to be locked really, except at midnight. And both Mammaws loved all of the company!

The progression of the cancer, however, was slowly taking its toll.

Creeping in, ever so slightly, there were changes occurring daily. At first, Mammaw came into the living room to watch television and visit. Then, a small ramp appeared to facilitate the step down into the living room, making access easier. Soon, the visits were accompanied by tubing, from the oxygen tank, that stretched along the floor, until, eventually, the recliner went to her room, and the visits were in there. Then, the wheelchair and walker became extensions of her movement, before, finally, the bed was her comfort. None of these changes were easy, but, still, she handled them with grace and laughter. At night, one of us always stayed in

My Gift to God

the recliner in her room, in case she needed anything, and really just to be close to her for as long as we possibly could.

One day, she and I were alone in her room. Everyone else was either sleeping, or had gone out to take a break, and she quietly confided in me, once again. Her appetite was dwindling, and we were fixing anything she craved in hopes to keep calories in her. I had been sitting in front of her, helping her eat some oatmeal, when she grabbed my hands with hers, and stopped me with urgency.

She said, "I have to talk with you, Sarah Jane." To which I replied, "Okay, Mammaw."

She opened up, telling me she knew her time was short and she was beginning to see things she knew were not there. She confessed to hearing things she discerned were not of this earth and although she was ready to go to Heaven, she was scared. Once again, I witnessed these tiny streams slip down her sunken in cheeks, and it was all I could do to stay composed. Squeezing my hands, with the little strength she could muster, she made me promise once again not to tell the others. She did not want them to be upset or watch them cry. My little Mammaw was, once again, trying to protect everyone, as she knew how scared everyone was. Once again, she relayed to me she was conveying her confidence because she felt I could handle it, although she knew I was scared also.

All I was thinking, as she sat there cradling my hands, squeezing them with the little bit of strength she had left, was, that she was the strong one, not me. I was thinking, "God, I do not know if I can do this.

This is my Mammaw.

This is my best friend.

This is the woman who has loved me, no matter what.

How could she possibly think I was strong, when my heart was buckling in my chest?"

She then started asking questions she did not want to ask. She had not, up until this point, allowed herself to ask, "Why? Why do you think this is happening, Sarah?"

My heart broke, as I sat there looking into her slightly cloudy eyes. All I could say was "Mammaw, I don't know. I don't know why this is happening. It makes no sense to me at all. I do know that you going through this has brought our family a lot closer together, but, gosh, I don't know if that is really a reason, much less an acceptable one. Momma and I can be in the same room now without wanting to fight all day, which is good, but it shouldn't take all of this for that to happen. So, I don't know why. I don't know why you are the one having to suffer." She said she did not know either, but she would not want any of us to have to suffer, like this.

I wrapped my arms around her and we just held each other for about five minutes, as she slowly brushed my hair, until she told me, "Don't forget, you promised. They don't need to worry."

My Gift to God

Several days after that, I traveled to Alabama for work and my Aunt Vonda called to tell me I needed to come home. She said, "I am not positive what is going on, but she is just different today. She isn't worse, she actually has more energy, but she is different and you need to come home." I wrapped up my meetings, quickly, and headed back as soon as possible. Adam and I had talked that afternoon, on the phone, and he had asked if he could meet me there, to which I agreed.

It was all very strange that day though. She, was different. And, did, in fact, have more energy, but what was strange, and what has left an impact on both Adam and I, from that day until now, was her description of what she was seeing and the look in her eyes while describing it. Her eyes had become cloudy over the past several weeks, which the doctors attributed to the cancer moving to her brain. But, this day, her eyes were not cloudy at all. In fact, they were bright and shining and she had this wonderment on her face. Earlier in the day, my Aunt Vonda and Aunt Carla told us she had asked they wheel her down by the creek that ran in front of the house. She had not been outside of her bedroom in close to a month, but she wanted to go outside and she was overjoyed and childlike while out there. This same excitement was still evident, although she was lying back in her bed, when both Adam and I arrived.

As I sat beside her on the bed, and Adam stood by the window,

My Mammaw

she started explaining to us she was seeing all these people come into her room. She was watching her mother and father, children that had passed away, among other individuals that seemed to be wanting to visit her. Then she described, in grand detail, this beautiful, magnificent, colorful tree. She expressed whimsically these colors on this tree she had never seen before.

The look of transfixion on her face and the clarity with which she was speaking, is still astounding to me, today.

Her words had been jumbled in recent days, but not, this day.

This day, she was witnessing Heaven from this earth and she was visiting with angels.

If ever my faith needed convincing there was a Heaven and a God, it was restored that day fully! I wish I had a recording of her description, and that conversation.

I do, however, have it written on my heart.

Adam and I did not ask her a lot of questions, we just listened to her talk until she had nothing else to say. Quietly, she drifted off into a slumber, with the sweetest, most peaceful smile I had ever bore witness to, up until that moment in my life.

Afterwards, Adam and I took a walk down by the same creek she had been wheeled out to, earlier in the day. I sat in the grass, while we talked for a few brief moments, and then he let me sit in silence, while tears gently rolled from eyes. We both knew the time was drawing near, and also, we could not put words to what we had just witnessed together. I am thankful Adam was there with me, and also, that my Mammaw loved people the way she did. Because, Stacey had called to come visit as well, on a different day. Much to my mother's disagreement, and expressing her dislike willingly, my Mammaw agreed to the visit. I knew Mammaw and Stacey did love each other, so, she did come for a very short visit. Although she and I did not speak in great length, that visit did provide some final closure that was peaceful.

There was continued reconciliation, as Mammaw asked someone call my Pappaw. They had gotten divorced many years ago, and although they had both remarried, they still held an affection for each other. He came to visit one afternoon and, she did not want anyone else in the room during that time. They visited for over an hour and, although none of us know what was spoken about that day, all we do know, is when he exited the room, there were tears in his eyes and on his face. He has since passed on as well, so I guess we will never know.

It is ironic though, that two days later, on my birthday, would prove to be the last day I would ever hear her say, "I love you" or speak in any audible words, at all. Then, one more week passed, and I found myself lying in her recliner next to her bed, when she took her final breath on this earth.

I know we will all never understand why, but the effect her sickness and dying had on our lives, and our relationships, sustains, even until today. She showed us, even in those last days, how much reconciliation meant.

The last week was trying, as we witnessed her body and breathing dwindling. We sat by her bedside, reading and singing to her, because those were the things she loved. The night she passed away, after everyone had gone to their couches or bedrooms to sleep, I sat on the edge of her bed, with her hand in mine, and sang hymns to her.

I brushed her hair and softly whispered against her cheek that we would be okay. "We don't want you to lay here and suffer Mammaw. And, I know you don't want to leave us and, gosh, we really don't want to do life without you here, either, but if anyone deserves Heaven, and to enter those Pearly Gates, it is you, Mammaw. You have suffered trials and tribulations and still brought us so much joy. You deserve to run on those streets of gold and play under that magnificent tree. Please do not toil here any longer, just for us."

I prayed aloud, "God, please do not let her suffer any longer."

With that, I sang Beulah Land, as I lay beside her and kissed her cheek. Then, I curled up in the recliner to watch her softly lying there. About two hours later, I drifted off slightly, but awoke suddenly, and when I did, I heard the last breathe, she would take here on earth.

I sat very still.

My Gift to God

Waiting.

Hoping, for one more breath.

Ten seconds, then twenty.

Still, nothing.

I got up, sat beside her, and placed my hand over her heart. There was nothing.

She was completely still. I closed her mouth, brushed her hair, took her hand in mine, and sat there several minutes, in the silence. I knew the chaos was coming, as soon as I left the room to do what she had asked me to do those weeks earlier, when she said, "Please, take care of the others."

I prayed a prayer, slowly got up, walked to the door, and stood there a minute longer. Lingering at the doorway, grasping the wall so I would not fall to the floor, before going to first my Aunt Carla's bedroom, then my Mother's couch, and lastly Aunt Vonda's couch, to utter the same words to each of them.

"Please wake up, she is gone."

Those were the hardest words to leave my mouth, and they are still the hardest words to believe. We called my Aunt Lynette and Uncle Jackie, before calling hospice and the funeral home. Those early morning hours were foggy, inside and out, sitting at the dining room table, writing out her obituary while watching the hearse pull down that long foggy driveway. Those memories are not easily erased.

My Mammaw

The impact of her life on my own is so strongly woven into my heart, and during those months after the diagnosis, during treatment, and prior to her death are some of the most intricately laced moments of the Holy Spirit, so sweetly, residing among us all. Everything else fell away, and it was all about her. She never was one for the attention, or to be the center of things, but in her sickness, everything else, to all of us, just stopped, nothing else mattered. Relationships, work, money: none of it mattered.

Loving her was the focus.

Making sure she was comfortable and not alone was the focus.

No more self-centeredness, at least for those last few months we had with her. She taught us so much. She taught me so much, and although I wish I could say there was this radical change in my life because of her dying, it did not happen that suddenly. It still took nearly a decade for me to figure out what she had been trying to teach me, all my life.

CHAPTER 9

Successful Running

《 —∞— 》

WITH THE DEATH OF MY Mammaw, an unsatisfied spirit was ushered in once again, as I was unsure of where to turn to. During her last year, I had begun dating Amy, one of the sweetest girls I had ever met. She was there through all of the highs and lows and had been putting up with my obstinacy, prior to Mammaw's diagnosis. Although I am uncertain of why she hung around, she did, and she especially helped during those last few months when I needed an escape. She would, intuitively, take me for a drive in the country, with nothing but music and the wind in our faces. On my birthday, she realized the need to release some adventure into my life, with all that was going on. She arranged for a beautiful afternoon of hang-gliding, before delivering me back to sit with my Mammaw, and listen to her utter those soft, feeble words, "Happy Birthday, Sarah. I love you." for the last time, ever.

For all accounts, Amy was the most stable and kindest person I had dated. Although I was completely on a roller coaster during that time, she would sit, and hold my hand, and pray with me. But, I was still floundering. In the months after the funeral, I felt rather dead inside, but instead of turning to alcohol or drugs, I started going back to church and working extensively. In fact, I had just been offered a business development position with an Indianapolis-based company, who held government consulting contracts. I accepted the position excitedly, prepared to leave all I had been experiencing as of late, behind. I found a way to run away again, but this time it had the means in which to actually run away and disappear, so I did not have to face the reality of my Mammaw's absence. I lived in a nice hotel suite in Indianapolis for six months, while in training for my new position, before being assigned my designated territory. Traveling home once a month, gave opportunity to take care of personal affairs and to make sure my dad had all that he needed. Jeff, a trusted friend, was living at my house, to take care of it and my dogs, as well as checking in on my dad, periodically. My life seemed to be turning the corner positively, with the exception of my relationship with Amy dwindling, because I was choosing to leave it all behind.

In addition to being in Indianapolis, there was a lot of travel with coworkers to client sites all over the Midwest to Missouri, Iowa, Minneapolis, Nebraska, and Illinois. It became a very busy time for me. Acclimating quickly to my new environment, I was meeting new people and developing long lasting friendships. In March, it was decided I would relocate to Kansas City, MO, in the crux of my new Midwestern territory, the first week of July. The challenge, however, was traveling Monday through Friday and only being home on the weekends. Attempting to get my house ready to be sold, buy a new house, and preparing my dad to move, was relatively exhausting. Also in the midst of this, I had the brilliant idea to begin a new relationship with a girl I had known for some time, named Laurie. She knew I was going to be moving, was always up for an adventure, and she decided she wanted to go as well. Not sure how I would handle being in a new town where I knew absolutely no one, I said, "Why not?" This meant she had a house to sell and a job to find, as well. It was chaotic and I was, literally, only home seven to eight days a month.

By the end of April, all of the changes were collapsing in on me. One Sunday, after much contemplation, I decided to go back to the church I had attended as a young girl, to hear my godfather preach. His sermon was about Joshua and owning the land where your feet are planted. As far as the sermon goes, that is all I remembered, but, what I specifically remember about that day, was praying this prayer to God:

"God, I have a lot going on and I don't know if I am supposed to go to Kansas City or not, but if you want me to go, you are going to have to make it happen, because I am going to back out! I am overwhelmed by all that has to happen. My house is not on the market, I don't have my dad's things ready to go, and I am supposed to leave in two and a half months. I'm not packed, I don't really want to leave my mountains to live in MO, of all places, so I am just saying if you want this thing to take place, you are going to have to make it happen, because I don't know how to."

That was my prayer and I meant it!

Apparently, He knew my heart, because I got home that afternoon and had no more stepped into the house, than my phone rang. It was Adriana's parents, who lived in Florida. I had not talked to her mom in some time, although we had a very valuable friendship, and she had no idea I was preparing to move, or that I had taken a new job. Before we even began discussing those things, she said to me:

"We were talking the other day and have decided if you ever decide to sell your house, we want to move to Tennessee."

My, jaw, hit the floor!

I was, like, "You have to be kidding me. You are joking, right?!"

She expressed that this was not a joke, and they were completely, serious.

I then explained about my new job, and she asked, "How much do you want for your house?" Not having thought about it, I just picked a number out of the air, and she said, "Okay. We'll be up there in a month. If you will get with a title company, we will buy it and you can stay there until it's time for you to move. We will even watch after your dad so you can get everything set up for him at your new house, and give you time to come back home and get him."

Just, like, that, everything was done.

It was finished!

God snapped His fingers, the phone rang, and I had no more excuses.

Every, single, legitimate, concern I was facing, was answered, by one phone call.

It was astounding!

Laurie's house, also sold, one month later, and she found a job before the move, as well.

We bought a big, beautiful house together, with a downstairs apartment in it for my dad, and that was it.

Bye-bye, Tennessee, Hello, Kansas City.

But, boy, did I not know the ride I was about to step onto! Even with God's hand so evident, I would still become a rebellious little prick.

The next several months still proved to be hectic, with buying the new house, saying our goodbyes, preparing for the movers to arrive, and beginning our trek half way across the United States, by car, to embark on this new life together. Moving day was filled with both excitement, and fear. I had never lived outside of Tennessee, but the anticipation of what was next was enough to encourage my adventurous spirit to move forward, full speed ahead. Driving to Kansas City, with our animals and two vehicles loaded down, was so fulfilling to me.

My Gift to God

Finally, a true get out of dodge was taking place. Although I had always been interested in moving, my dreams always involved larger mountains, such as the Rocky Mountains of either Colorado, or Utah, not the flatter lands of Missouri.

I really believe God was playing a trick on me, because the mountains had become such an escape for me, over the past five years and, had replaced my church life. My thought was that I could experience God more outside than in communion with other people. And now, here I was, moving to a city where the closest mountains were twelve hours away, in either direction, east or west.

If you do not believe God has a sense of humor, trust me, He does!

I will never forget the feeling of pulling into Kansas City for the first time, as residents.

Here I was. Here we were.

I had arrived!

We had arrived!

New City.

Driving a brand new BMW.

New 3500 Square foot house with a three car garage.

New job with a six figure income.

New relationship.

I was home.

Succesful Running

Everything in my life was now new, and I could leave everything else behind, and I do mean everything.

Laurie and I set out, to create our life together. After the movers had delivered our belongings, we prepared the downstairs for my dad's arrival. Some friends of Laurie's had driven from Tennessee to help with what renovation needed to be completed. Then, I made the flight back to Tennessee, to pick up my dad and fly him out. Amy was still very much a part of my life, as we were trying to transform a relationship into a friendship, and she picked me up from the airport and drove me and my father back, the next day. Out of all the things and people to say goodbye to, she was the most difficult. But, she had not wanted to leave her family, which I completely understood. Again, you can see there was this element of game playing going on in my life.

I liked and cared about Laurie, but I loved Amy. However, Laurie had wanted to go to Kansas City, whereas Amy had not. My decision processes had clearly not improved much, but nonetheless, I was determined to make it all work out, somehow. Even though what I desired, and my satisfaction, was leading the charge.

Although Laurie and I attempted to build a solid relationship, and from the outside it appeared we had one, it was on shaky ground from the beginning. We began making friends quickly in Kansas City and began hosting dinner parties and taking trips with friends, so the adventurous side of both of our spirits was satisfied, but, still, some things were lacking. We even began attending church together, which, in itself, is a comical God story. While traveling home from a client site visit, two weeks after beginning life in the city, I was on the phone with Adam discussing anything and everything, when the subject turned to church. He asked if I had found somewhere to attend yet, to which I replied, "No I have not. And I really do not know how I am going to go about that."

The city was so big and whereas I was used to the south where churches were, literally, on every street corner, it was different in the Midwest. There is definitely a church presence, but it was not in your face, as it was back in Tennessee. It had also been difficult to locate a church within the denomination I grew up attending. I had looked in the phone book and done some limited searching, but came up empty handed. I had taken for granted that there would be one, primarily, I believe, because my hometown was residence to the international church headquarters. I had not realized, until that point, how sheltered I really was. It took me a long time to get used to the fact that, upon introduction to a new person, the first questions you heard were not,

"Where do you go to church? And where did you go to school?"

These were expected answers to be delivered back at home, so people could figure out where you came from, what kind of person you were, and if they knew any of your family. I had no idea I had lived my life in a community that immediately stereotyped everyone

Succesful Running

based on these answers, with no real consideration to anything else. But here, in this new city, came the challenge of finding a church community, and Adam began to try and help me.

Adam then asked if I had ever attended a Vineyard church, to which I replied, "I am not sure I even know what that is."

At that very moment, I came around a curve on I-35 South, and there, directly in front of me, was a big church with beautiful stained glass windows. The setting sun beamed through those windows, like a beacon. The name on the sign read, Harmony Vineyard Church.

Laughter filled my car as I explained to Adam what I was staring at, straight away in front of me, and it was only about fifteen minutes from my house.

Perfect!

That was on a Friday, so Sunday morning, I went to church by myself. Everyone was very friendly, but more importantly, was the interesting fact that the preacher preached from the same text my godfather had been preaching from the day God answered my prayers about the house selling.

Own the ground where your feet are planted.

That was attention grabbing enough, but then after the service was over, I was leaving my seat, which was near the back of the sanctuary. I wanted to slip out quietly, when all of a sudden I saw Pastor John coming off of the stage, and it appeared he was in a hurry. He told a couple of people, who tried to stop him, to hold on a second and as I was turning down the aisle, he touched my arm and said:

"I am sorry to stop you, but I have to speak with you."

Surprised, I said, okay, and he shared that this was really unusual behavior for him and he had no idea who I was, but that God instructed him to come and tell me I was exactly where I was supposed to be and I did not need to search any longer.

He said, "I do not know if that means anything to you, because it is rather ambiguous, but I got the message loud and clear."

This was the place I was to call home. And, he was correct. This was where I was supposed to be.

God, lovingly placed me in the arms of a church family, where no one knew me. Under the care of Pastor John Brown and Pastor James Harris, I would learn, what the love of Christ truly looked like, within a church.

I had been used to being in churches where everyone knew everyone, and they knew my entire family. Although hushedly not speaking directly of my lifestyle, they knew I was "living in sin with women" and any time I would go to the altar to pray about something, they assumed that was what I was praying about. After any given church service, where I did visit the altar for prayer, I would continually get comments such as:

"We are proud of you and we will be praying for you too," or

"Whatever we can do to help you to get better, you know we are here."

These were limited conditional prayers based solely on what they "thought" I was praying about, when, more often than not, what I was at the altar praying about had nothing at all to do with my homosexuality. As far as I was concerned, God and I had come to terms with that since he had not taken it from me when I had given him permission to, all of those years ago.

How naïve I was in my thinking at that time, but more than all of those comments were the times I felt like I had a report card from church. Those times I would go to the altar to pray, I would no sooner get home from church, than a phone call from my mother would be received. Listening, as she would tell me, "How proud of me she was, that I went to the altar today."

Each, and, every, single time, this happened, the more infuriated I became. Not just at her, but at the church. I had become angry and untrusting.

Despising that I had a report card every single time I darkened the church doors, closing my heart off to the church became effortless. Statements laced with condemnation and masked as prodding concerns into my personal whereabouts, I began enduring lavish amounts of statements, when I had not attended church in a while, such as, "Well, we haven't seen you in a while. Why haven't you been here? Where have you been?" or "We've been praying for you," with an awkward silence, staring at me, in anticipation of an answer, afterwards.

But, the most infuriating, was after being at the altar on any given Sunday to hear the words "I am so proud of you." It made no sense to me, because what, exactly, were they proud of? There was no inquiry of what I was praying about, it was always an assumption about what I "should" be praying about.

Even to this day, I believe Jesus meets us all, individually, and He deals with us on certain aspects of our lives in His timing. If we do not allow Him, the space, for people to be touched and allowed to converse with God, without being curious as to what we think they need to be praying for, then we lose the battle of leading people into their own relationship with Christ.

Because each experience is so unique and individualized, we cannot begin to comprehend the works that Christ is doing in someone's life, or in their heart. And, this is precisely where I had been for years, within my church family. It was more of a family, when I was being good, and coming to church. Other than that, there was no involvement or interaction, whatsoever. Initiation began and ended upon me entering or leaving the church doors. And, yes, I could have attended other churches, seeing as my options were endless in my community. However, in my experience, the interactions would have not been much different, and I desired to be

Succesful Running

among those who knew me, even if it was superficially, that they understood my heart.

But, here I was in Kansas City, MO, where the only people I knew were Laurie, my dad and my neighbors. And, after talking with Adam, I had found myself in a church where no one knew me, but yet I was known, and invited in with no questions and no reports to be made. I am unsure of how long I attended Harmony Vineyard, before Laurie began joining me at church. This was a new experience for her, as she had not attended on a regular basis, since her younger childhood years. However, when we would attend, we chose to sit on the very front row and worship until our hearts were content.

Now, please understand, my heart was genuine, but the condition of my heart was not. I loved to worship and, to this day, I long to close my eyes and picture myself walking up to the gates with thanksgiving and entering the courts with praise, until I can see my Father God sitting on the throne in majesty.

I get lost quickly, in the image.

One Sunday, during our morning break, between worship and the message, I saw Pastor James on the far side of the sanctuary hurriedly leave his seat and take the stairs into the balcony, and it grabbed my attention. I watched as he moved quickly behind all of the people to come all the way to the other side, and down the stairs that was near our pew, in the front of the church. He walked directly to where Laurie and I were standing, looked me dead in the eye, and said,

"God sent me to tell you that His Spirit is all over you. You are His daughter and you are anointed and, more than that, you are loved."

Now, this was a bit awkward, with Laurie standing there, as this had turned into a conversation between just him and me. Tears welled up in my eyes, as he stood in front of me, grasping my hands and my feet felt insubstantial to preserve my position.

Here stood this pastor, speaking life into a girl's heart that had been so hurt by the church and, who was longing to just belong. This one moment was a confirmation to my heart that I was safe in this place and I could begin trusting again. These people did not know me, yet, they loved me.

Laurie and I continued to attend on a regular basis, even as the blustery winter months approached, but our relationship with each other began to falter. For whatever reason, I began to feel like her mother, rather than her partner. She desired to go out more on the weekends than I did, which would turn into verbal confrontations when I wanted to go home and she wanted to stay out. Now, this is not meant to paint me in some type of angelic light, because I was actually beginning to resent her. I began resenting that she wanted to do everything I wanted to do, and I felt the only reason she did certain things was because I was doing them. One such instance that, to this day, makes me angry at myself, was a Sunday morning when I was getting ready for church.

This particular day, I did not want her company at church. With no word or discussion explaining where I was preparing to go, she asked if I was going to church, to which I sarcastically replied,

"Of course. Where else would I be going?"

She then proceeded to tell me she would get ready and join me, to which I vehemently, sighed, and said, "Fine!" A small argument erupted as she asked me why I did not want her to go and I self-righteously conveyed,

"Because you only want to go because I am going! Why don't you ever want to go by yourself or find your own church to go to?!"

This, of course, upset her even more and she explained that she really did just want to go, and I sarcastically told her,

"Fine, but you better hurry because I am leaving in twenty minutes!"

Hateful and accusatory, I emphatically challenged her for no other reason than I knew people were starting to catch on that we were a couple, and I did not want to get kicked out of church or face judgment, as had happened before.

The amazing thing about that day was not anything on my part, however. I immediately began beating myself up for being so mean, although I did not say a single word to her on the ride to the church. When we pulled in the parking lot, I had this overwhelming feeling I

My Gift to God

had to apologize to her, before we went inside. Before getting out of the car, I just sat there in silence for a few minutes while she stared at me, like, well, aren't we going inside? Wrestling with my thoughts, I turned sideways in the car, grabbed her hand, and apologized, genuinely, for being such a jerk. I did not want our argument, or my stubbornness, to interfere or distract us from going in, worshiping, and hearing Gods word.

And, I meant it.

Intending to not revert to my past experiences and be the cause of someone missing out on His goodness because we were too wrapped up in ourselves, I knew this resolution was necessary. We gave each other a hug and kiss, and off into church we went. The astonishing thing, was what happened after we left. I do not remember the message or anything from the service that morning, but Laurie probably does. After church, we got back into the car and she asked if I minded pulling into a park that was just down from the church, so we could take a short walk. Sensing something was up, but unsure what it was, we walked to a bench in front of a fountain, and sat down. With tears streaming down her face she turned to me and quietly spoke,

"I, think, I am ready."

I had no earthly idea what she was talking about, as she continued, pensively,

"I, am ready, to give my heart, to God."

With wide eyes, I looked at her, because I did not know she was not saved. She began sharing with me that she would attend church with her Gran in her younger years, before her family moved to Tennessee, but she had really never asked God into her heart. Now, she knew that she was ready, and was asking me to pray with her.

At this point, I was flabbergasted she wanted to do this, and that I had no idea she was not saved. Also, I had never led someone in a sinner's prayer for forgiveness. How could I do this after being such a complete jerk to her, just two hours prior?

Those next few minutes seemed like hours, as we knelt on the ground. I completely submitted the prayer to God, because I had no clue as to what I was doing, or why He would have the day work out like this. I am thankful, though, that no matter what we do in our ugly human nature, He can, and does, always turn it around, if we listen to Him. To this day, I feel unworthy to have led her in that prayer and, at times, I feel like a hypocrite because it was not too long after that, our relationship ended. I am glad to say her relationship with God, did, and does, continue and, in fact, I had nothing at all to do with it!

Laurie and I remain somewhat friends today, although our breakup was less than ideal. We attempted to stay in the same house, together, for several months, although living in separate bedrooms, because we both owned the home. Eventually, she moved out into an apartment. About a year after our split, we did try to work things out and although we cared about each other, there was just too much missing. Up until my move back to Tennessee, from Kansas City, we had to remain in contact because of financial obligations, but even that began to strain our friendship. We both became protective and only afforded the truth of our situation to the very closest family and friends, although we both maintained our own sides of the story.

After Laurie moved out, I experienced a different sense of freedom. For once, there were no ties to a relationship, nor, did I desire one. I wanted to be alone, and I was not seeking to keep anyone's company. I began filling my time, when not working, with interests I had always wanted to pursue, but had not felt I had the capability to do so in the past. But now, with my freedom and success both pretty secure, it was easy. I began taking piano lessons, and bought a baby grand because that is what you should learn to play "Mary Had a Little Lamb" on. I also had some friends who were involved in the local theatre scene, so I auditioned and got some parts in some productions, which introduced me to a whole new love. My adventurous side was continuing to be fed by becoming certified in scuba diving, and I began traveling once or twice a month on weekend dive trips, across the country and into Mexico. In the midst of this also, I took a class to get my motorcycle license. So for all I could say, life was pretty darn good.

Even in work, I achieved success quickly, becoming known among my territories and was sought out, repeatedly, for job offers by my competitors. Even church was going well, as I no longer had a relationship to keep secret, although it really was not a secret, remember I liked to sit on the front row. Becoming more comfortable, I got involved with some small groups and joined the choir. Harmony Vineyard was really settling in as a church home to me. To solidify that even deeper, during one of the monthly communions, Pastor James asked his daughter-in-law to ask me to join in communion with his family. This was such a gift, that day. Typically, the communion was taken as families huddled together, but I usually just knelt down and prayed by myself. This particular day, Sarah, his daughter-in-law, came to get me. When I joined them, he shared that he and his wife, Wanda, had spoken and prayed about this, and they felt God wanted them to ask me to join their family, not just for communion, but truly as a member of their family. I was so completely blessed that day by that offering, but what I did not realize was, he did not take that as lightly, as I did.

He felt God truly spoke to him that I was to become a part of their family. To this day, they treat me as a daughter, although it took me a long time to understand what God was doing, and what He is continuing to do.

At that time, however, what I felt was a protection and an unconditional love. James will tell you, even now, that God told him that I needed a family to love me, and that was it. He knew I needed love and that is exactly what they did, then, and what they continue to do. God truly did place me in that church, with people that He knew I was going to need, especially when I entered the next part of my life. I needed safety and, although I would turn from it once again and turn away from them, they continued to love me as their daughter. That is a love that only God can place in you. God was still pursuing me, surrounding me with people who would care and lift me up in prayer continually, no matter where I would walk on this earth.

CHAPTER 10

The Devil's Intimate Blow

《 —∞— 》

WITH NO ONE TO HOLD ME back, I experienced much success, and began relishing the time I was spending alone to explore all the city had to offer. When the longing to spend time with someone on a regular basis would creep up, I ultimately decided to transfer the desire into areas of adventurous opportunity. Attending church more regularly at Harmony Vineyard, I was beginning to seek some solace there and, with no company in tow, I began trying to fit in and find my own space in the church. I was also beginning to feel this tugging within to try and clean my act up and be a "good girl" once again. I still saw my friends outside of church, but I was not drinking as much or going out to the clubs. Having found a new love for the arts, and having been cast in two plays, at a local community theatre, it consumed a lot of my time with rehearsals, and then practice at home. And when I had breaks, I would take off on whatever adventures came open with the scuba diving club or heading out to Colorado to hit the slopes, snowboarding. I was determined to keep myself occupied, which was easy with my job and then outside of work, I found the options were unlimited. A new frontier awaited, and I was ready to embrace it all with absolutely no restraints.

Desiring the life I always dreamed of, I relished an honest independence, seeking what my mom and dad had instilled in me as a little girl, with the dreams of success, God, and family all combined. My mother and I were in the beginning stages, once again, of attempting communication on a regular basis, and my dad and I were able to spend a great deal of quality time together, with just the two of us in the house now. For nearly a year, these became the accolades that I sought and developing these new perspectives felt sensible and stable. But, a new day was just beyond the threshold.

Unchartered territory arrived after an elementary classmate, Brian, contacted me. I had not spoken to him, personally, in many years although we had been around each other periodically while I was in a relationship with Stacey. She had been close friends with Cindy, the mother of Brian's daughter. The two of us were often present when he would come to pick up Kaitlyn for the weekend, or at special occasions, such as her birthday party. In fact, from the time she was just under a year old until the age of eight or nine, we spent many days babysitting Kaitlyn, having slumber parties, changing diapers, playing dress up, and riding four wheelers or dirt bikes with her, that she and her mother were, literally, extensions of our family. Kaitlyn was now twelve years old. It was really good to hear, from Brian, how much she had grown, over the past few years.

Soon, after that first conversation, and establishing common ground, Brian and I began talking daily, even though he still resided in our hometown. It was really quite surreal. We did not have any physical visits for many months, however, we became an integral part of each other's daily lives. As the months carried on and the conversations became more frequent, I curiously planned a trip back home to visit. Reunited with Kaitlyn, as if no time had elapsed, Brian and I were able to spend some quality time together, in person. It was very easy for all of us because we already had a history and relationship with one another. It was confusing to Kaitlyn's mother, that Brian and I were somewhat dating, but, heck, the whole thing was confusing to me also. I had moved into this mentality that, somehow, if I could clean my act up, stop partying like a rock star, become a good daughter, go to church, and date a guy, that I could be acceptable again, to my family, to the church, to my friends, and that all would be good. I tried, real hard, to be "good," to slough off all that could potentially separate me from living a good, perfect life and, so hopefully, I would find some normalcy and protection.

Things seemed to be progressing pretty well with this plan. After several months of talking on the phone, I made a first visit back home to visit Brian, where we decided to pursue a relationship.

My Gift to God

Then I made a second and a third trip, and we had plans for a week's vacation with the three of us, in the Caribbean.

Then, the devil decided to interject, at precisely the right moment, to deliver a blow, I had no sight on at all.

I was traveling from a work conference in Indianapolis, back to Kansas City, where Brian was flying in at the same time from Tennessee. We had discussed the potential of him moving to KC and, since he had never been there, he wanted to visit for a week and feel things out. While at the airport awaiting my flight, he called and said he was not going to be able to make it. He explained everything was okay, he just could not be away from home. I completely understood, although a little disappointed, and we made plans to change his ticket to come in a few more weeks, prior to us leaving for our cruise.

A few days later, I wrapped up performances at the theatre and accompanied some theatre cohorts, to an outdoor venue, to see Fiddler on the Roof. Brian called several times while I was there, so I stepped away towards the concession area to return his phone call. He started asking me questions to see if I was familiar with certain people from back at home in Tennessee. He had gone to dinner with some friends, and they started discussing our relationship. Apparently, there were some people there I had known a couple of years prior to moving to KC. I explained to him I did, in fact, know them while I was dating Stacey, but did not go in to great detail, as he already knew all about my past relationships. We then excitedly talked about our trip in a couple of weeks, and that we both could not wait to spend the time together, just the three of us. He even made a joke about us getting married while on the ship, or on the beach, and I replied,

"Well, you never know. But, for now, the intercession will be over soon. Can I call you back when it is over?" To which he said, no problem.

Afterwards, I tried to call a few times, with no answer,

Several hours later, I called again, and still no answer.

I was getting a little concerned, but with the time difference, I thought maybe he just went to bed early. That was unlike him, being a night owl and all, but benefit of the doubt was all I had. The next morning, I tried to call, since it was normal to talk when we woke up, but his phone went directly to voice mail.

Now, I sensed something was terribly wrong, but I did not have much time to focus on it, because I was doing laundry, getting my dad situated, and packing to leave for another work conference the following morning. While zipping my suitcase, my phone rang at 5:30 that evening. It was him. He fed me some line about where he had been, but I could hear the difference in his voice.

He began telling me he was not sure if things were going to work out between us. Surprised, I replied jokingly,

"That's funny, seeing as that's not the conversation we were having yesterday evening when we were joking about getting married on our cruise."

He then launched into asking me questions about Kaitlyn, his daughter. Hesitantly, he began with,

"You know, Kaitlyn is getting into her early teen years. What do you think will happen when she begins to have questions about certain things as teenagers do? What will you do?"

Confused, I responded, "Well, I guess that is really up to you and Cindy, as to what questions you want me to answer, or if you want me to defer back to the two of you. But, Kaitlyn and I do have a trusting relationship, so I hope that she will be fine and comfortable coming to me, if you want her to."

I did not know what else to say, and my response seemed pretty logical in my mind. Then, he threw out another one,

"Well, what about when her body starts developing. What will you do?"

Not understanding what he was saying, I asked for clarification. And the punch, was delivered, as he spoke these unforgettable words,

"Well, what will you do when she undresses in front of you?"

The devil hit me, straight away, between the eyes, and with, that, one, question, my heart was ripped wide open! Bleeding and exposed, there was no protection. Ripped open to the core.

Vulnerable, with no-where to hide.

It, literally, took my breath away!

In that one, tiny little sentence, he called me a pervert. And, although he heard the hurt and the tears in my disheveled voice, as the tears were streaming down my face, like a broken faucet, he spoke his parting statement, "It's just not going to work" and with that, the conversation ended.

Forever.

Those, were our last verbal words to each other, even to this day.

But, what the devil did, was, he used Brian to deliver, on a silver platter, a blow to destroy me.

Everything, became void of any feeling, once again.

No longer wanting to feel!

No longer trusting anyone or anything!

I, wanted, destruction!

I started, immediately, vehemently, seeking ways to disappear from everything that mattered.

Concern meant nothing, and I ran to deeper and darker places than I had ever experienced before.

There was no hope evident.

I had tried to be good. And, I had failed.

Nothing, was ever, going to be good enough.

I, was never, going to be good enough.

My Gift to God

I remember sitting down on the side of my tub, the phone still in my hands, and tears streaming down my face, silently, screaming inside my chest, making an impenetrable vow to,

NEVER.

EVER.

ALLOW.

THIS.

AGAIN.

I was finished with feelings!

I was finished with God!

Finished!

It was finished!

No more relationships that had any feeling.

No more friends that could become closer than I had control over.

I dove into finding my escapes from everyday existence. Work, became my first god, because I knew it was all up to me. I always went above and beyond and made good money doing it. Drinking, became my second god. It was allowed, and even expected, at the government conferences I attended, for weeks at a time, entertaining clients, and then while at home, I had a score of friends to pull from to drink with. Drugs, became my third god. They were easily accessible among the crowds I once again began running with, and, most of the time, so available that it did not cost me anything, to snort lines of coke at a party, take some pills, or smoke some weed. Whatever my pleasure, I could find it in my hands in minutes. Sex, became my fourth god. Mainly with women, because that was easier, but occasionally with men as well, because I needed a release, and I desired control. A fifth god entered slowly into the mix when I was lonely and not constantly surrounded by friends and my other gods. That god, was bulimia.

I could, not, stand myself, so now, not only did I desire to destroy my external existence, but also my internal one.

I cannot recall the first time that I did it, but I can tell you what it did for me. If at any point, I began to feel emotions of sadness, I would eat until I could throw up

to forget,

to not feel,

to have control.

I learned, how to do it quietly. I learned, what foods were best for it, or easier. And on weekends or especially on holidays, when everyone else was with family and I felt the most alone, I would stop at the grocery store and purchase two bags full of my "special mix" of foods. Knowing full well, I planned to go home, cook what needed to be cooked, and then eat, and throw up.

Eat again, and throw up again.

The vicious cycle could last all day if I wanted it to.

Anything, for an escape. Anything, for control.

My Gift to God

I then started applying that to when I went out drinking. I would drink to intoxication, hardly eating anything at all, but I did not like passing out, not at first anyway. I learned, at what point I needed to purge in order to keep going, to still be able to drink, and maintain just enough control, but not enough to feel anything.

It became a very dangerous, balancing game.

The combination of the two, alcohol and bulimia, was intoxicating to my emotions, but it wreaked havoc with my internal body systems. Today, I still deal with some of those residual effects. But, in the midst of all of this, I did not care about those things. As long as I still had my job and could go do whatever I wanted to do, whenever I wanted to do it, then I was doing all right.

Today, I am amazed that I even survived without more detrimental factors affecting me.

In fact, the drinking and bulimia started rattling out of control when I began dating someone that was doing the exact same things. She called me out on it one evening when she had stayed over at my house. Eventually, because we knew each other's secret, we would even go to the bathroom to throw up together, and then go drink some more, until we had finally had enough and went home to have drunken sex, before passing out, awaking the next morning, to start the games all over again.

Once again, the one thing I said I would never do was turn into my father, and there I was, doing exactly that! Now, I understood why he became an alcoholic, and sought that escape from reality, and no longer did I blame him for doing any of it.

It made perfect sense.

Rationale of these activities became deceptively easy to discern for me. Even more so because in that vow I made while sitting on the edge of the tub, that unforgettable night after hanging up the phone with Brian, was the vow to Never let God determine my actions again.

He would be separate from me, because He had not protected me or cared enough.

Somehow, I rationalized that He had not taken feelings from me, He had not protected me, and He had now allowed this man, who I thought was a Godly man, to hurt me so intentionally that I would not forgive God for it.

No longer did I have any desire to even open my bible, much less attend a church service, even for special occasions. And, although I could easily discern the deceptive spirits I was engaging in, I thought I would find more solace there, than I ever would with God.

Not only had Brian hurt me with his words, but God had hurt me by not protecting me.

This was my mindset, and I welcomed the devil and his dominions.

I ushered them, into my house.

My Gift to God

Into my bedroom.

And into my body.

All for the sake of just not wanting to feel, much less to be among the living.

The only thing that kept me from seriously entertaining the thoughts of suicide, was the thought of who would take care of my dad if I was not there, because I was all that he had.

I could not see past the blinders to understand I was doing such a poor job of caring for either one of us that it didn't really matter if I was around or not. I was so absent in mind and body, but, nevertheless, he was the only thing that kept me from choosing which avenue I wanted for death.

This attitude carried on for the better part of a year, and over time, crept to extremities that there was no turning back from, in my mind. I had made very definitive choices and had carefully surrounded myself with those who enjoyed the destruction and games as much as I did. Continuing to allow people only so close, but not too close. While I dated several women over the period of this year, I really desired their company more to avoid being alone than desiring a real relationship, and in my good fortune, that is all they sought as well. As the drinking steadily increased, I was unable to realize I was dangerously close to losing control of the games, until one Sunday morning I woke up in a bed, in someone else's house, and I had no idea how I had gotten there.

This had happened before, but this time was different.

When I woke up, I was alone and, I remember opening my eyes and lying there very still. I looked down my body and there was a blanket over my legs, and I was lying on top of the bed covers. Fully clothed, I could see my shoes neatly placed on the floor, beside the bed. My winter coat was folded and draped over a chair, with my other belongings very neatly lying beside it. The house was not one I recognized and was very large, with extravagant furnishings. I put on my shoes and gathered my belongings, before walking around the house to try and figure this all out. I looked in a couple of other rooms and no one was there, so I went downstairs to the living room, and there was a guy on the couch, passed out, whom I did not recognize. I went into the kitchen, fixed myself a drink of water and looked on the counter at some mail to see if I recognized a name, and I did not. I then went back towards the front of the house, down a long hallway and there was a bathroom that I could see light spilling out from underneath the door. I opened the door gingerly, and there was a woman curled around the commode, with her pants around her ankles, and although she looked slightly familiar, I could not see her face. No one that was there even flinched, they were so passed out.

I looked at my phone, it was 7am on a Sunday morning and I had no idea where I was. When I walked outside, I had no idea where my car was. So now, I had no idea how I arrived at this big beautiful house, nor did I know where my car was. I started walking down the

My Gift to God

street in the bitter winter air to try and find out the general vicinity of my location. The mail on the counter had been addressed to a P.O. Box, which proved unhelpful, and had now commenced my scavenger hunt for road signage. I walked down this long hilly road until I found an intersecting street sign and dialed my friend Julie's number. She was the only person who I thought might be awake at this hour on a Sunday. She arrived at the corner intersection about fifteen minutes later and, then we retraced what few steps I could recall from the beginning of the evening the night prior, until we found my car sitting in the parking lot of the second bar I had been to. We then went and had coffee and breakfast, laughed about what had just happened and then I went home to recoup before my coming workweek.

You would think this would have been a wake-up call, but, in fact, it was becoming normal behavior and almost a game of feeling indestructible, once again. What I realize now is God was protecting me from so many things that could have gone wrong, at any given moment, while I was dangerously spinning the chambers of the guns of my gods.

I was playing my own version of Russian roulette. And, even when one of my friends, Jessica, asked me why I was "acting out" and seeking things she knew I did not really want, I just brushed her off as a silly girl who did not know what she was talking about. But, she was absolutely correct in her observation.

The Devil's Intimate Blow

I was acting out and my circumstances or impending consequences bore no real truth to me at the time. The escape was what I was after. I wanted to be finished with it all, and so, I carried on, traipsing down whatever destructive path that enticed me at the moment. It was a very dangerous game.

Some nights, or mornings if you will, when this would occur, my car would be outside and I just had to drive until I figured out where I was. But, I cannot tell you how many instances this occurred and I was never raped, taken advantage of or had any wrecks, even though I had no recollection of how or why I had arrived at my locations. All I can tell you is I did not want to be home, and I did not want to be alone in the physical, although I was very alone, emotionally.

CHAPTER 11

Flirting

« —∞— »

I AM UNSURE OF WHAT PARTICULAR event happened, or if multiple occurrences coincided, but it became evident I was unraveling, and my body was severely affected, physically. Facing the reality that I was a violent bulimic, meaning when I ate it would not stay down whether I wanted it to or not because my digestive system was so out of whack, accompanied with the alcohol and drugs tanking my immune system, I began feeling very ill. At one point, a doctor, without knowledge of the bulimia, diagnosed me with early stage cancer, although they did not have an origination pinpointed. I started antibiotics, steroids, along with other medications, to no avail. Having a severely depressed immune system, accompanied with a low tolerance for prescription medication, these options left me feeling overtly tired and destitute. Unwilling to share my plight with anyone, I internalized everything I heard my doctor say. With no resolution to the cause of my sickness, and my unwillingness to be transparent with my physician, I eventually just cancelled my treatments, appointments, and medication. There was no purpose in trying to pinpoint what was wrong, when all along, I knew my own self-destruction was the underlying root cause.

One particular Friday evening, not long after the many doctor's visits, for some reason I had nowhere to go and all of my regular cohorts seemed to be busy. I refused to go home, just to stay there and be alone. After contemplating what I wanted to do for the evening, I found myself driving down the stretch of interstate I had first seen Harmony Vineyard come into view, while on the phone with Adam, several years prior. Once again, I rounded the same curve on the interstate, and there it was, in plain sight. The lights were on and cars were in the parking lot. It reminded me on the first Friday of every month, they held a worship night. Spontaneously, I decided, "What the heck. I don't have anywhere else to go, and at least I won't be alone." So, I exited the interstate and pulled into the church parking lot.

I sat there for the longest time, watching as people walked inside.

Some people I recognized, and others I did not.

Unsure of why I was really sitting there, I knew I did not want to talk or interact with anyone. I was simply contemplating slipping in for a couple of minutes and alternately slipping right back out, without any grand entrance or exit.

Flirting

It seems I sat in my darkened, silent car for the better part of forty-five minutes, contemplating whether I was actually going to go inside, or find somewhere else to go. I kept checking my phone for returned texts or calls.

Nothing. Silence.

Silence in my car.

Silence from my phone.

My head was swarming with questions and thoughts.

"What the heck are you doing here?

You have no place here.

You walked away, remember?!

You could go down to Harry's and just sit at the bar. You know someone is going to come in that you know and you won't have to be alone very long.

You know if you go inside everyone is going to look at you and ask what you are doing there.

You don't belong here, remember?!

You know they will be judging you, so why bother?"

Over and over, these questions, tangling in my mind. At one point, I even pulled out of my parking space and was headed for the exit, but somewhere deep inside there was this longing to go inside.

So, slowly, I found another parking space. Quietly, I got out of my car and just stood there holding the door handle, still unsure.

My Gift to God

Finally, after about ten minutes, I walked gingerly up the sidewalk to the door, looking to make sure I would not run into anyone and have to talk. Upon getting closer to the door, I was happy to see the door greeter step away down the hall. I hurried in so I did not have to encounter her, either.

No one in the hallway, I crept to the far side of the church and stood looking in at the sanctuary, still unconvinced I would take a seat. Normally, I would have been the person that went to the front pew, no matter what time I got to church, but no more did I want to be recognized. If I could have just curled up under one of the pews, that would have been fine with me.

I wanted to be there, but I did not want to be seen.

Another ten minutes went by, and I slipped into the sanctuary, sitting in the back, as far from anyone as I could get.

I do not recall what they were doing besides playing some worship music and people were singing and praying. I sat in that pew, dressed in my bar clothes, wishing I was somewhere else, even though my feet would not move me, and I was scared.

Keeping my head low and trying my best not to be recognized, all I could focus on were my inner thoughts and feelings. I kept telling myself I had no business being there and these people do not even know me, anymore. None of Pastor James' family was there, and even if they had been, I would have expected them to ignore me, as I had ignored their phone calls and messages to me. I had not

Flirting

wanted to give them an opportunity to reject me. Instead, I had chosen to stay away, and to remain silent to them. But, no matter what my thoughts kept provoking in my mind, I could not move.

I felt bolted to that pew, although looking for an opportunity to sneak back out, without triggering any noise.

No prayers or singing were uttered from my lips, only silence.

The longer I sat, the more uncomfortable I became. Eventually, someone asked everyone to stand in prayer, and I thought, this is my opportunity to escape without being noticed. Waiting until everyone closed their eyes in prayer, I exited my seat and walked quickly to the vestibule door. And there before me, stood Pastor John, and with everyone else being quiet he gives me a big hug and exclaims jovially,

"I thought I saw you back here! How are you doing?"

I was flabbergasted as he hugged me tightly and spoke excitedly with no admonition or judgment, only a sincere relaying that it was so good to see me and, hopefully, we see each other again soon. He never looked down at what I was wearing, he looked me straight in the eyes with a glint of happiness.

With a big smile and a warm hug, he asked if I was leaving and when I replied affirmatively, he opened the door for me out into the hallway with a grin and an invitation to come back anytime.

In all of my church life, I had never experienced what he had just delivered.

My Gift to God

Always, after being gone from a church for a period of time back at home, I was each, and every, single, time met with accusatory eyes and words of,

"We haven't seen you in a long time. Where have you been? Why haven't you been here?"

Never was it, "How are you doing? It is so good to see you. Oh, you are leaving? Well, let me get the door for you. You know you are welcome here anytime."

I stood in that hallway for a good ten minutes, as I watched him talk to others. Perplexed, he never once tried to get me to come back in and sit down, or make me feel bad for leaving. Intrigued by what I had just experienced, part of me wanted to go back in, although I did not, at least not that evening. Having received a text message from some friends, I rushed off to meet them at a bar. But, even that was unsatisfying that evening, because I could not take my mind's eye off of what I had just experienced.

I wish I could say this captured moment changed my life, but, in fact, it did not. However, it did strike a stirring spark to come back closer to God, and to "try" church again. At least that was what I had in my mind to do, to "try." It did not happen straightaway, but over a couple of months' time, I would visit on Sunday mornings, occasionally. Even though I was beginning to re-enter the church, I did not feel worthy at all to be there because for the most part I was

Flirting

still doing all of the things I had been doing over the last year, but now I was throwing churchgoing back into the mix, once again.

This time was different though. Instead of sitting on the right side of the sanctuary, all of the way on the front row, I was sitting on the left side, towards the back. This may appear silly, because you would think it would not make a difference, but for me, at that time, it did. I knew I could sit there and not have to be seen by many people. And, because it was the section behind where the pastors and elders typically sat, if I left early or came in late, they were less likely to know.

But, there was another reason also. I would not readily admit it, however, I felt like I needed extra protection. That may come across as funny to some that I sought protection by sitting in close proximity to the pastors, but it was something I felt inside. With everything I was involved and participating in regularly, I had become a part of more darkness and was more easily influenced by it, than I was actually comfortable with. Although, not yet willing to give it all up, I did feel if I had this extra protection, somehow, I might remain safe. Now, I do not think that is what kept me from so many potential harmful things occurring, but for whatever reason, it did provide a sense of security.

The hard realization about this season of my life, is that I was flirting.

I was flirting with absolutely every area of my life that I could.

My Gift to God

I was coming to church, but only just enough.

I was dating people, but only just enough to not have commitment.

I was working hard, but playing with my job opportunities.

I was flirting with relationships with my family, just enough to maintain contact, but not enough to get hurt.

I was even flirting with the devil, doing things I knew were not of God, but clearly of the devil. I flirted, as if to say, "You can have me, but only this much, because I am going back to church on Sunday. I will get my protection for the week. Then, I will leave church to go meet up with my friends and do whatever I want for the rest of the week, but I will be back next week to get another healthy dose of protection to keep me treated enough to carry on doing all of the things I desire. You can have me, but you can only have a portion of me."

This was a very dangerous condition to be playing with, but I did not care. I figured I had it all, now.

My family where I wanted them,

My friends where I wanted them,

Work where I wanted them,

The devil where I wanted him,

And, lastly, God, where I wanted Him.

Flirting

Each had their designated spot in my life, which I could control and walk easily from one to the other, with no effect on the other as long as I was in control.

No one thing could overpower and take me down any longer.

I was protected from every angle.

Or, so I thought.

CHAPTER 12

Adam Visits

《 —∞— 》

SOMEWHERE AROUND THIS TIME, Adam was calling. I am going to backtrack for a minute to provide some context and clarity. The summer I was preparing to move to Missouri, Adam called and asked to stop by my house for a visit. I will never forget that May afternoon. He was one week away from getting married. Although we had maintained contact over those last several years, and he had been around when my Mammaw passed away, our relationship had not moved from a friendship since that birthday dinner many years ago. We maintained a respect and kindness for each other, although he always desired more than friendship. I was too self-involved to allow that to happen and because I respected him and believed I would defile him if we were to move further than friendship, I made sure to keep him only so close.

But, this May afternoon he walked into my living room, took a seat in a rocking chair across the room from the couch I was perched on and began asking questions about my marriage to Dawson. He wanted to know how I knew, on the day I was marrying him, it was

My Gift to God

the wrong thing to do. I explained to him, I just knew in my heart. I knew it was not in God's will, but yet I did it, anyway. He then proceeded to tell me he was not sure if he was supposed to get married, the very next week. Dead silence lingered heavily between us as he sat there staring at me, after unloading those words. We both knew what he was really saying to me. He wanted to know if there was ever going to be a chance we would fulfill all of those prophecies. And, I never shared with him what I heard God speak to my heart that birthday evening, when we were outside beneath the stars.

We both just sat there, not knowing what to say in the most awkward, but, simultaneously, quite comfortable silence. He knew I was moving and I knew he was getting married. I could not tell him not to marry her, because I also could not make him any promises that we would ever move further than friendship. So, silence filled the room as we quietly sat there, staring at each other. We each knew both of our lives were about to make a drastic turn; mine in another state and his with a wife. I will never forget when he stood up to leave, from that rocking chair in my living room.

His hands were in his pockets, intently looking at me, while bidding me good luck with my move. I told him he could call anytime, although I was not sure how much help I would be.

We laughed slightly, with a long silent pause following, before he said, "I guess I better go." And I replied, solemnly, "Okay."

Adam Visits

I never moved from my position on the couch.

There was no hug, or handshake.

There was nothing, but an awkward "I will see you later" and with that, he walked slowly out the door and I watched him drive away. For over an hour I sat in silence, unsure of what had just taken place, or if it had been the right thing to do.

Now, fast forward a few years and he was calling for advice once again, this time, about his marriage in jeopardy. Many things had transpired while I was in Kansas City. Not long after my move, his father was involved in an accident at work and passed away, due to a major head injury. Adam had called during that time, as well, because he knew I had experienced Mammaw's final breathe and, with the test results having not delivered good news, Adam bore the weight of the decision about the ventilator.

Subsequently, he experienced monumental adjustments in his life and his marriage had not escaped the suffering. His questions this time involved how he could save his marriage, or if he should even attempt to. Without digging into the specifics of their relationship, my advice to him was to try everything, at all costs, to save the marriage so there would be no regrets on his part, no matter what may happen in the end.

Looking back, it is curious to me I gave him that advice, because of my tumultuous train wreck of a life at the time. But, I understood enough to know that, more than anything, he would not want to have regrets. I delivered the most unbiased, honest advice possible and although they attempted counseling, and other things, eventually they filed for divorce.

Nearly six months passed and, we had begun talking on a more regular basis, just about life, as friends. I told him about Brian and the conversation that threw me into a tailspin, and his response was one I will never forget as long as I live.

After I unpacked the entire conversation, with tears trailing down my face, once again, I recollected how that final question from Brian about "What if she undresses in front of you?" affected me. Adam very calmly and matter of factly, whispered to my heart with these words,

"Sarah, if that is really what he thought about you, and if that was truly a concern, then he never really knew you. You know that, right? He never knew your heart."

Adam, in that one brief moment, gave my heart the validation I needed, because this was not something I had shared with anyone else. He heard the hurt my heart had been punctured by, in that cataclysmic conversation with Brian, and was able to reinstitute truth into the very core of me. Although we were over a thousand miles apart, he was right there with me.

Again, I understood that he just got me, and understood me, like no other.

Adam Visits

After several more conversations, he made his intentions known. He wanted to come to Kansas City for a visit, but I told him it was not time, yet. He was still newly separated and, although divorce papers had been filed, I understood, from experience, there was more to divorce than paperwork. Even though the divorce was mutually desired, the emotional ties needed time to pass before the introduction of anything else. I, once again, put him at arm's length, the difference this time was that I did not want to.

On the phone one evening, after leaving a client event, a few months later, I told him, "I think it is time. If you want to come visit, I think the timing is good." We had no more ended the conversation than he found a plane ticket and by the time I arrived back at my house, the ticket was booked.

He would visit the week of his birthday, the first week of September.

I was excited for his arrival as it had been several years since we had seen each other face to face. In the days leading up to his visit, I was more of a nervous wreck than I had ever been with anyone before. You would have thought I did not even know him, and while driving to the airport to pick him up, it would have been comedic to watch me.

I drove around and around the airport, trying my best to figure out what I was going to say to him, when I first saw him, and trying to decide where I was going to park, so we did not have to walk very far. His flight was slightly delayed when I arrived at the airport, which gave me more time than I needed to just walk around.

I am pretty sure I sat in close to twenty seats near where he would exit the terminal, trying to find the perfect seat. Still having no earthly idea what I was going to say to him, or if we would just give each other a big hug, or if would we just stare stupidly at each other.

I had so many questions and thoughts going through my mind.

I wonder if he still looks the same.

I know I probably look a little different.

What all are we going to do when he gets here?

I had absolutely no idea!

I then saw the computer screen change to indicate his plane had arrived, and it was at the gate. My nerves became unbearable for this normally cool, calm and collected girl and it was more than I could stand.

I was sweating.

I went to the bathroom.

I came out.

I sat down in one chair. It seemed too close.

I moved to another one, but it seemed too far away.

I stood by the glass, but that seemed too eager.

So, you know what I did?

The most outrageous thing you could possibly think of!

Adam Visits

I walked over to the ticketing counters, and no one was there, because it was the last flight of the evening. Along the wall, there were two big garbage cans, side by side.

I walked over and proceeded to squat on the left side of one of those big blue garbage cans, so no one could see me. He, as well as all of the other passengers, would be walking away from me, towards baggage claim. There would be absolutely no chance for me to be seen, as they walked past!

Those final moments of nervousness, led me to crouch beside a garbage can! Ridiculous. Hilarious.

Even now, it makes me smile and laugh inside to know my sweet Mammaw really was right on, when she said "That boy has an effect on you, Sarah!" Even in those moments, beside that trashcan, I probably still would have said to her that she had no idea what she was talking about. But, apparently it was the truth!

I squatted there and watched people walking by, trying to catch a glimpse of him, first, before he discovered my whereabouts.

And then, there he was. Dressed in jeans and boots, with a white button down on, carrying a bag. I could see him looking all around, turning side to side to try and find me, and all at once my spirit took a big sigh . . .

Deep breath in, deep, slow, deep breath out.

Peaceful.

My Gift to God

I was not nervous any longer. Unsure what I was going to say to him, nevertheless, I watched him turn around, take one final look down the corridor and start walking towards baggage claim. I let him get a little ways ahead of me, watching him walk for a minute and then I sauntered up to him, on the right side, slowing my walk to meet his stride and said to him,

"Hey stranger, how are ya doing?"

Finally, I got to see him again. He grabbed me in a big hug, although later he kidded me that I had stolen his opportunity to walk off the plane and plant a big ole kiss on me, before I could say a word. But, I had thwarted his plans while crouching beside a big, blue airport trashcan.

The weeks prior to his arrival had been filled with long hours of conversation, yet, here we stood beside each other and neither of us knew what to say.

It was classic!

Adam will tell you that walking up to the car was when he got nervous. I go walking towards this black BMW, clicking the key fob, and he was wondering where my little Honda Accord went to. Then, after driving through the city, we pulled into the driveway of this gigantic house with a three car garage and he was wondering where was that little hippie girl he used to know in Tennessee, who was always on the river or off somewhere at a concert. Walking inside, he saw the baby grand piano in the entranceway and was

Adam Visits

certain that we must be at the wrong house. A lot of things had changed, for both of us, over the years.

But, no, this was the right house, with the right girl.

That week flew by as we got to know each other, all over again, in person. The changes in our lives began to collide and to usher in the ways we had both evolved in the past several years. By the end of that week, we believed we wanted to see where this would go. He had made contact with a potential employer during his visit and was offered a job, so, in one month he planned to return, and stay for the winter season. We decided we would see where things went, from there.

In October, I flew home to Tennessee to see family and to ride with him back to Kansas City. You would have thought by the reaction of our families we were getting married, not just beginning a relationship.

My Aunt Vonda, in particular, said "It is about time!" They had known from the beginning, just like my Mammaw had, that Adam and I cared for each other. My mother, on the other hand, was ecstatic for an altogether different reason.

She was excited that her only daughter, was finally dating a guy.

Even though she liked Adam, it was more the other aspect that she was excited about. The day we were leaving, she had decided to host a dinner at my Aunt Carla's house, so the family could "just all get together." This was so far from the actual intention of that dinner, and was completely evident to everyone. There were people there I, literally, could not recall the last time I had been in their presence. In the midst of all of the chaos, one of my cousin's husbands, Virgil, relayed to Adam and I,

"Well, it seems the only thing we are missing is the preacher, because this is like a wedding reception." And, he was dead on with that statement.

That is precisely what it seemed like. Everything was going pretty well until mere moments before our departure. Adam and I were loading up to go tell his mom goodbye, before hitting the road for our twelve hour trek to Missouri. We were standing in the doorway and my mom grabbed me for a big hug goodbye, as she announced,

"I am so glad you are better. I am so glad you are fixed."

Appalled, everyone else in the room disappeared, along with the smile on my face, as I asked her what exactly she meant by that statement. She tried to recover and said,

"Well, you know, I'm just glad you are with Adam."

Horrified that these words were coming from my own mother, I rebutted, "I did not need "fixing." I am not "better", as you say, because there is nothing wrong with me. Every relationship I have ever been in has made me who I am today, and I am not sorry for that and have no regrets. I cannot believe you think this about me!"

Adam Visits

She tried backtracking and my aunt Vonda told her there was really no other way what she said could have been taken, and with that I told her, "I love you, but I have got to go."

I was livid when I crawled up into Adam's truck, and as we pulled away, all I could think was,

"What the hell just happened, and why?"

I knew my mother and I still did not see things eye-to-eye all of the time, but I had no idea we were this far off from each other. I thought, somewhere along the line, we had come alongside each other in some commonality. Especially after Laurie and I had just moved to KC, she and two of my aunts had flown out for a visit and spent four days with us, in our house, under the same roof. There had been no problems then, but, now . . .

I felt like our relationship had just taken a giant leap backwards and once again, I was becoming obstinate towards her.

Adam and I left on our grand adventure, half way across the country, traveling the same roads I had been on years prior, on my way to Kansas City originally. I would like to say we drove off into the sunset and everything was sunshiny and rainbows ever since, but that was not true.

Once again, Adam was ready to settle it all down and although I was ready in my mind, I was not ready in my heart or maybe that was in my heart and not in my mind. I will let you figure that out. I did not realize what a toll my independence had taken on my life,

My Gift to God

and how much of a stance I had taken that things were my way or the highway. I had made my life to be a certain way and I still wanted to do whatever it was I wanted to do. I just wanted Adam to join me, in whatever endeavor that may be at the time.

He humored me for a while, dining at fancy restaurants and wine bars, letting me adjust his wardrobe to what I thought would look good on him, while also taking in the theater and symphony. Although some of these things he very much enjoyed this was so far from his lifestyle the conclave of the two was preposterous. His idea of going out to eat was fast food or Waffle House, not all of these fancy restaurants. My idea of grocery shopping was vegetarian, organic and soy, while his was meat and potatoes and frozen dinners.

Once again, our lives were colliding and it might as well have been a fight to the death, because my way was always the best. To be clear, we did not fight, and even to this day, we are not confrontational people, especially with each other. We stand for what we believe in, but unnecessary fighting is not how we are wired.

So eventually, he began doing his thing and I began doing mine, which is not a good combination when starting a new relationship.

Now enter into the picture I had taken a new job and Laurie was my co-worker. We saw each other at work several days a week and sometimes on a daily basis, and had reunited as friends. Soon after, she took a job to transfer back to Tennessee and my feelings all

Adam Visits

began to stir about. I was trying to reconcile this new relationship with Adam, with Laurie and me spending a lot of time together. Then, she was moving back to where we came from, together, and leaving me in this big city.

Confusion launched into my heart because when we had moved to KC we thought we would never leave there, unless we left together. Now, I was the one that had to stay behind, when it had been my previous job that had led us here in the first place. Adam was not very happy with my despondency, indecisiveness, and, in effect, emotional distance I was placing between the two of us. One particular day, we had gone hiking and he had made his mind up that either I came around that day and we worked it out, or he was throwing all of his stuff in his truck and heading back to Tennessee, that very evening.

I had no idea this was his plan, and am thankful God woke my heart up that day. I sincerely apologized to him for all of my abrasiveness and disregard, and asked for his forgiveness. It was then he told me he was glad I had taken the time to actually look him in the eyes, because I had not done so in weeks. He also informed me of what his plans had been, when we returned from the hike, if something had not changed while we were gone.

All I can say, is God intervened when I could not, or would not, do it on my own. I realized, in that moment, how self-consumed I had actually become. The weeks became better and soon the papers

My Gift to God

were delivered that Adam's divorce was final, but I was still so unsure of which way was up. More pointedly, I was not sure of what I was willing to give up in order to pursue this relationship, full on, with him.

I did not want it to cost me anything and although we definitely cared for each other and were going to church together, our connection was beginning to fizzle, due to my lack of concern for anything I did not want. You can call it whatever you want, but the best word I have is self-absorbed, and unwilling to release my heart, or to trust anyone, even Adam. At the end of that winter, his seasonal job had come to a close. Although they offered him a part-time summer position before coming back in the winter full-time, he knew he could go back to Tennessee and have his former full-time position back, immediately.

So, that is what he did.

When he left, we had no clear direction on where our relationship stood or even if it did. We never had a break up, once again, but neither one of us really knew exactly what we wanted. There were no definitive plans of when we would see each other again, or if we would. Nor were there definitive plans of him coming back in the winter. In fact, he had no intention of doing so. It was really bizarre, looking back on it now. We talked every day for a while and then even that began dwindling as there was an attitude of what was the point. One day while on the phone, I told

Adam Visits

him I was making plans to visit some friends in Florida and did he have any thoughts about it. His enigmatic, truthful response to me was,

"Should I have a response? Because it does not seem like I should have a say in what you do or what you don't do. So, I guess just go and do whatever it is that you want to."

Things had really come full circle, now.

So, I did just what he said. I began to do what it is that I had learned to do best, whatever in the world I felt like doing. Although this time, fortunately, it did not involve all of the drugs, just the drinking and adventure.

CHAPTER 13

Surgery
« —∞— »

UNTIL ONE DAY!
I was at work and began feeling ill. Knowing something was wrong, but not understanding the gravity of the pain, I stepped away to call a friend, who was a nurse, and explain my symptoms. Her response,

"You need to go to the hospital, immediately."

After a quick discussion with my employees, one of them offered to accompany me, with great objection on my part. But, I was in no condition to drive, so they delivered me to the emergency room, at the local hospital. Immediately, I was taken back, with my blood pressure sky rocketing through the roof and the nurse drew blood as it spewed across the room. I was hunched over in excruciating pain and after administering painkillers into an IV, a plethora of tests were then performed. The doctor came in to deliver the unexpected news of my condition. He began by explaining that, during the ultrasound and MRI, they discovered ten tumors in and around my uterus, and he asked if I knew about them.

My Gift to God

I was in shock, because all I heard was the word tumors and then was wondering how I could possibly know this information. Tumors? Tumors?! That was all I could hear. I thought he was preposterous!

The doctor then tells me, nonchalantly, they are called fibroid tumors and not to be worried because they may or may not be cancerous, and an emergency appointment for the following Monday, with the best Obstetrics Surgeon in the region, had been made for me. Leaving with more questions than I entered the hospital with, and then told to go home, relax, and try not to worry for four days, was even more ludicrous. They sent me home with pain medication and the newfound knowledge that I was carrying ten tumors with me, along with another one that was apparently in the process of degenerating and instituting this resonating pain throughout my body cavity. It was Thursday afternoon, and all I could hear in my head was,

"Am I dying?? Tumors?? Really?? Four days. I have to wait four days!"

Sent home to painfully wait out those incredibly long four days, I arrived at the doctor's office Monday morning carrying all of my test results. Immediately, after reviewing all the information and performing an intense examination, she delivered even more unsettling news, "You need surgery, as soon as possible."

Surgery

This was really not the information I desired to hear from her, especially because the timing could not be worse, remember I liked things on my timeframe! But, also, my step father was in the last stages of life with lung cancer, and I had a trip planned in one week to see him, and help my mom out. I was also planning to visit Adam, to determine if we could make heads or tails about where our relationship stood. But, now, my doctor was sitting in front of me saying we have to get this done as soon as possible.

We discussed alternatives, and although she was willing to send me for a couple of tests to see if I might be a candidate for a less invasive type of surgery, than cutting me wide open, she really did not anticipate this being an option. I opted for the testing, then left for my trip to Tennessee, with an appointment to see her immediately upon returning, to review the findings.

While in Tennessee, Adam and I had a good visit, although nothing had been solidified, as far as our relationship was concerned. With so many miles separating us, and the future uncertain as to where my location may be in the near future, it was unsettling to him. I was being groomed for a significant promotion that would require a move to an undetermined location, within the next six months. With too many unanswered anomalies in our conversation, as he drove me to my Mom's, we determined there was still no long term commitment, other than caring about each other's lives, until further decisions were rendered.

My Gift to God

Visiting my Mom and Larry brought some much needed closure to Larry's and my relationship. Considering the state of the relationship with my mom, he and I did not have much solid ground to stand on in the first place and we had never really seen eye to eye on much. However, this time spent together facilitated us making amends and giving voice to words that needed to be spoken.

To back up a little bit and give context to the relationship, my mom and Larry had dated when she was in high school. My grandfather had been a minister at a little church in the town they now lived in, but he did not approve of their involvement. As a result, during my mother's senior year of high school, she was sent to live with my great-aunt and uncle, which is where she, eventually, met my dad. Almost thirty years later, one month after my marriage to Dawson, my mom returned to that town to visit a high school friend and was re-acquainted with Larry. She came home from that visit in November and divulged that she had been reunited with an old flame and they were planning to be married the coming January. She also announced she would be moving to a small town in Indiana, where he then lived.

When I separated from Dawson that May, Stacey and I made a trip to Indiana. Both my mother and Larry were suspicious of our relationship, and we just did not get off on the right foot with each other. Nearly a decade would pass before Larry and I saw each other again, when my Mammaw passed away. And now, here we were,

Surgery

trying to make amends in his last months of life. We wholeheartedly succeeded in voicing a resolution that at the core was held together by the concern from both of us, for my mother. Although our relationship was strained, he knew I loved her, and although he and I had not had an ideal "step" relationship, I knew he loved her also, and she loved him. Nothing else needed to be said, we had reconciled through love.

With the tying up of some loose ends, I returned to Kansas City at the end of June and awaited my visit with the doctor, that same week. She explained, during that appointment, I was not a candidate for the less invasive surgery, and in fact, the operation was going to be quite complicated. As she delved into the intricacies of the surgery, she explained the necessity of an additional surgeon to assist. Bombarded with the details, she then laid out several scenarios that included cancer and non-cancerous and what each of those circumstances would require, because they would not know, until they were inside, what they were facing. Accompanying the concern of cancer, another possibility loomed. Hysterectomy. If the tumors were all cancerous, the risk would be too great to leave all of my womanly parts, and the potential to carry life inside of me.

It was one more torturous blow to the torso, as I had always wanted to have children and desired to feel a baby growing in my womb. But now, hearing the possibility may have to be taken, I sat with tears rolling continuously down my cheeks and onto the notepad in my lap. But, God. He had placed me with this woman doctor who was not only my age, but who also shared my given first name. As she delivered the newest of news to me, she also offered her hands and tears, as she had not yet born children herself or been married, and knew why I was sitting before her with tears staining our hands. In that moment, she made a promise to me. She would do everything humanly possible to save that probability. But, even with the promise, signing the papers explaining that option and giving my singular consent, left me trembling inside.

We then moved on to discuss recovery and expectations. Unfortunately, what I heard and what she said were two completely different things. She informed me my stay in the hospital would be anywhere from three days to one week, depending on which approach would be taken. The extensiveness of the surgery would determine the recovery time also, and would be anywhere from two to three weeks on bed rest, up to twelve to fourteen weeks with complete restrictions. However, what I heard, was I was going to have surgery with two very competent surgeons, that I would be in the hospital for no more than three days, and I would be back to work in under one month. Never having had anything, other than knee surgery, complicate my life for an extended amount of time, I was prepared to remain in control and prepare myself physically for an optimal recovery time. My expectation was that this was to be

Surgery

merely a speed bump in the road, in which I would need limited assistance, and nothing further.

Interviews were rapidly approaching for my promotion, so I informed my doctor the earliest I could do surgery was the last week of August. She did not believe waiting was a wise idea, as she enlightened me to what I would be experiencing over the next two months while putting this surgery off. I remained adamant that I had to get my life in order to be away for a couple of weeks. Although not in agreement with my decision, she could do nothing but accept my arrogance. I believed, I could handle the discomfort and pain for two more months.

We then scheduled the surgery, for August 24th.

July was a mad rush of interviews and preparing my team at work for my departure, while also ensuring my dad was taken care of during my hospitalization and my mother arranged to travel and be with me during my time at the hospital. I thought everything was coming together nicely, although I was still uneasy, and experiencing a great deal of pain. However, two weeks before my surgery, Larry took a turn for the worse and passed away, so I traveled back to Tennessee for his funeral. Resolute not to have the focus turned towards me, and to be there, emotionally, for my mother, I attempted to conceal the physical effects of the travel.

It was precisely as the doctor had predicted.

My Gift to God

Adam drove to be with me the last day I was in Tennessee, and also drove me back to the airport in Nashville. This was, in essence, one of the most awkward times we had ever spent together. He was attempting to convey his thoughts that possibly we should just remain close friends, as I divulged to him that, from my standpoint that was no longer a prospect. Too much had happened and although we could try and tell ourselves that was an option, I knew in the depths of my heart it was not. Our care, concern, and love for each other was too deep for friendship. Although it was apparent we had no idea how to be in a relationship, with the distance separating us, we determined we would just have to see what happened. For now though, I had to get back to Kansas City to make my final preparations for surgery. And, although that was the second most awkward goodbye we had ever experienced, we still had an uncertain future together.

Returning to KC, surgery and work preparations superseded everything else. I had one week left, and I was a nervous wreck. Final interviews for the upcoming promotion resulted in my selection for one of the top two positions available, and management had agreed to wait until I returned from surgery, in a month, before making the final decisions. My mom still planned to travel and thought it would be a good reprieve for her to get away for a week, while I was in the hospital and coming home.

Surgery

The countdown was on and now it was Friday, before my Monday surgery.

Mom was flying in Saturday night and would help me prep for surgery on Sunday. As the end of the workday approached on Friday, I realized I was a ball of nerves. One of my coworkers suggested we go out to have dinner and wine, ecstatically, I agreed. The invitation meant I would no longer have to go home and solely focus on the days ahead. Quickly, I headed home to change, explain to my dad I would be back in a few hours, and ensure he did not need anything, prior to heading downtown to a little wine bar we both loved.

I expected to call it an early night, as the next morning I had to put in a couple of hours work. My nerves were still shot, accompanying the now ongoing pain, and I was not very hungry, so I decided to simply have two glasses of wine. We left there and stopped by another favorite little bar, where I decided to just have water, since I had not eaten. We met another co-worker and, by this time, it was ten o'clock. I decided it was best that I leave, to drive the fifteen minutes home.

Driving up the interstate, I was less than five minutes from my house when I came up on a roadblock, diverting drivers off of the interstate. A gigantic operation, a combination of MO State Patrol/Kansas City Police initiative was taking place, and the entire exit was blocked off. I could see a school bus, accompanied by another large trailer and at least fifteen patrol cars.

I proceeded down the exit ramp, rolled down my window and began to speak with the officer who asked if I had consumed any alcohol recently. I told him the truth.

"Yes officer, I had some wine a couple of hours ago." He talked with me for a few minutes and then asked me to step out of my vehicle.

I had no idea the world that I was about to encounter, that would alter my course, and become an unexpected chapter in my life.

CHAPTER 14

Waking Up To Consequences
« —∞— »

STEPPING OUT OF MY PERFECTLY clean, black BMW and walking over with the officer, I was completely oblivious to what was about to take place. In high heels, I attempted to stand on one foot with my arms stretched out straight, without falling, and I could not. Feeling like a flamingo, I asked to take my shoes off and, with my bare feet on the warm, sticky asphalt, I attempted again and did okay. He then asked me to walk a straight line, one foot in front of the other, without looking down, and, once again, I did okay. The whole time this was taking place, I was thinking there was no way I would not able to pass this stuff. I happily complied until he explained I needed to step up into the trailer and take a breathalyzer, possibly answer some additional questions. Beginning to think this was all just a dream, I was too embarrassed to tell him my neighbors were detectives, and to see if that would make a difference. Instead, I just tried my best to be compliant, because I thought there was no way under the stars I would fail the breathalyzer.

My Gift to God

All of the occurrences of that evening were fresh in my mind, unlike other nights I had driven home or arrived at some unknown location with no recollection of even having been behind the wheel of my car. I really thought this would be a breeze and I would get right back in my car and be home in less than thirty minutes. Just another speed bump in the road.

Boy, was I in for a very, very rude awakening, and a dose of reality.

I stepped into that trailer and blew into the breathalyzer, twice, and then sat down to talk with another officer. He then informed me I had failed the tests, my car would be towed to the impound lot and I would be taken downtown to the jail. I was officially, under arrest.

My world exploded in an instant, as I sat there trying to figure out what in the world was going on.

What had I done?

How had I gotten here?

How was I going to get out of this one?

But, I wasn't going to be able to.

My reading on the breathalyzer was barely over the limit, but it did not matter. Realizing there were no excuses to be considered, they put me in handcuffs and led me out of the trailer. Across the road to the school bus, I had noticed prior to exiting my car, they escorted me up the stairs. Sitting in the seat was not a driver however, but another police officer, and the bus had been converted into a make shift jailhouse.

Divided into three holding compartments, each section was enclosed with heavy-duty wire walls and locking doors. Up front, by the driver, was one area with a single bench seat barely big enough to hold two people. A small aisle way divided the back down the middle, one side for women and the other side for men. Each of those two sections was equipped with several long benches, extending the length of the bus. After taking in my surroundings, I was transferred to the officer of the bus, with my belongings in a manila envelope. She accepted my belongings and logged me in, then she stopped and deliberately studied me for a few moments, before uttering to me quietly,

"I have no idea why you are here, but you don't belong here."

I just stared back at her with my eyes wide open as she continued and said, "I am going to put you up here beside me, so you are not back there with the others."

It was the strangest thing, sitting there, completely aware of everything that was going on, and just being very contemplative and quiet. I was not angry, and although I had questions running through my head, I was just, quiet. The fact that I was very aware and coherent, however, would not remain lost on me as the night continued or in the days to come. After several minutes, she asked if there was a cell phone with my belongings and if there was someone

My Gift to God

I could call, discreetly, without alerting the others, who all appeared to be asleep at the time. Quietly, but excited, I said, "Yes, thank you so much!"

She dug through the envelope of my belongings, produced my pink Blackberry phone and handed it to me, quickly. The first call I made was to the detectives that lived down the street. They informed me I should have called prior to the sobriety check and now it was too late. I was already logged into the system.

I then called Adam, no answer.

I tried the coworkers I had been with previously, again, no answer.

Phone call after phone call, no answer.

Then I called a good friend Sarai, whose boyfriend, Joe, was a bartender, because I knew they would still be awake. Finally, an answer! The accommodating bus officer relayed all of the pertinent information about where they would be able to retrieve me, what the process would be like for the next several hours, and approximately how long it would take if everything went quickly. I thanked her and Sarai repeatedly, and she returned my phone to its belongings. She then revealed that she was not supposed to do any of that, but she wanted to help me, and, again I expressed my heartfelt gratitude. Looking back, I am even more grateful she was obviously placed there to care for me before I entered what would be another eye opening revelation.

Waking Up To Consequences

The paddy wagon arrived and I quickly realized until that moment, my entire world had been one that was sheltered. My friendly officer led me down to this van that was separated front from back, women in front, and men in back with a small bar-laden window in between the two sections. Dreadfully tight quarters, another small bench seat awaited me, along with a girl who was already a passenger. They handcuffed and shackled her and me together.

No longer, was I separated.

I was bound. Handcuffs on my hands and shackled with chains around my ankles, I was fettered to a girl who was only twenty-two years old, but who was much more experienced at this life than I had ever thought possible at that age. For the next two to three hours, we were shoulder to shoulder. My arms subsisted as they were twisted behind my back and I was being physically pulled back and forth, as she would not sit still. Curious to her knowledge of this life, I listened, silently, as she conversed with two gentlemen in the back of the paddy wagon.

One remained rather subdued while the other exchanged stories with her, triumphantly, about their numerous times in jail and what they were going in for that particular evening, as we had all been picked up at various locations. The conversation then shifted into a counseling session as she began delivering advice regarding his circumstances and how to best maneuver the system, since he was a

My Gift to God

repeat offender, like her. I just sat there, still as a mouse, in my spirit and in my mind just taking it all in.

About an hour after being in this windowless, confined space, traveling what seemed like a hundred miles of unseen roads, while feeling like a fly on the wall of an insider's support group, we came to a very sudden stop. The officers we were unable to see in the front, jumped out and we heard a multitude of voices screaming and yelling. Then the back of the van popped open, and they threw another occupant in amongst us, who had been running from officers for quite some time, we learned. After they got him settled with his new companions, they slammed the door shut and everything turned into a ruckus. It suddenly got very loud as my wrist mate began exchanging information with him, as well as the other guy she had been conversing with. At this point, the conversation radically transformed and I no longer understood any of the slang they were speaking. For the first time, I realized this was serious business.

I was bound to someone, and I better pay close attention!

Still remaining extremely quiet, she never even acknowledged my presence, nor did it seem to affect her that she was joined to another person, in such an awkward manner.

Our paddy wagon was now considered full, so they drove us downtown to processing. Thankful this leg of the trip was coming to an end, I heard a big metal garage door open, shortly thereafter. Suddenly, we were descending below the street and then the van stopped with a jolt. We sat there for another ten minutes and, at this point, the brouhaha had ceased and none of my fellow occupants were talking or even looking at each other. They had all become substantially calmer and no longer did it feel like we were on a party bus, but rather like a sleep study group. Two officers then opened the doors and instructed us to hurry, get out, and not to take our time.

Here we were, this girl and I, still bound wrists and ankles, and I felt like I was in some freaky field race, with the exception of people cheering us on to win, we were being pushed to move faster with no reward at the end. Although this was not my companions first rodeo, I was learning on the fly how to walk shackled, in heels, attached to another human being who had complete disregard that anyone was beside her. Trying to be compliant and hurry without falling down, they loaded all of us onto a dimly lit, cold freight elevator and up we went about fifteen stories, until it jerked to a halt abruptly. They ushered us into a small holding room with bars and glass surrounding us. Girls on one side of the cramped room on a tiny bench and guys on the other side on their own bench, facing each other.

Now, not only were we shackled to each other, but we were attached to the wall so no one could move a single iota.

Still, everyone was quiet, just looking at the floor, until finally another officer came to retrieve me. Do you want to know what he said to me?

"What are you doing here? You don't belong here."

My Gift to God

Kindly, I smiled back at him, and said, "Yeah, that's what I keep hearing." He was very compassionate, reassuring me things were going to be okay and joking while he took my picture and fingerprints. He tried to make me smile for the booking picture, I respectfully declined, because that was definitely one camera I was not going to smile for!

It absolutely hurts my spirit to say I know what the booking process is like, or that I have a record, but consequences are consequences. What was happening that evening was my eyes were being opened, widely, to the effect of my choices.

No longer was I invincible, as I had always believed, and my ego was having some notches inexplicably removed.

After the officer completed the booking process, he delivered me to another station where I had to stand against a wall, empty all my pockets, and remove my jewelry and shoes before being given slipper socks to put on my feet. I was allowed to remain in my own clothes, which was a pair of grey pants and a white short-sleeve shirt. After all of my belongings were placed in a bag, with my manila envelope, I signed an acknowledgment, then they logged it into possession and escorted me down a long corridor of jail cells.

This, was nothing like what you see on television.

There were so many jail cells down different hallways, and smaller holding cells out in the middle of the hallway, barely big enough for someone to lie down in. As I was being led to my holding cell, we passed a girl curled up on the floor of one of the single cells. She was really loud and obnoxious, although no one seemed to pay her any attention. I turned to look at this curious sight, as she seemed to be spilling out of the cell, and the officer instructed me emphatically not to pay her any mind, and to maintain looking straight ahead, so I obeyed. We arrived at our destination, and she opened the door, instructed me to turn around and put my hands through the holding window, so she could unlock the handcuffs. For the first time since entering the paddy wagon, I was free again.

But, what I was free to walk into, was very disturbing.

There were bars everywhere I looked. Standing in a small corridor of the cell, with a grey cinder block wall to my left, on my right was a row of bars that served as a partition wall. Walking in about four feet, I stood in a common area, with a bolted down grey metal picnic table in the center of the room. A big black garbage can, in the far right corner, was chained to the bars so it could not be moved. About five feet above was a very small window, with bars on it, as well. A single telephone was mounted on the grey cinder block wall adjacent to the picnic table. While standing at the entrance to the common area, I could see to my right was another jail door that was closed and locked, sequestered with additional bars. It enclosed a smaller holding/common area and two cells that included six grey metal beds with no mattresses bolted to cement walls in each. Walking into the common area a little further, I found there were two other larger cells with no doors on them to the right with eight grey metal beds bolted to each of their walls on each side, sixteen in each cell. A single steel commode was located at the very back of both of those cells, and that was it.

I took it all in, very slowly turning my head to catch every angle and take stock of my surroundings as best possible.

In the separated holding cells, I was locked away from entering, were two girls who were talking to each other. In the common area, there were three girls on the floor seated against the cinder block and near the telephone. In the cells off from the common area, I could see the beds were all taken, and some of them had two people to each mattress-less bed. There were no benches other than what was attached to the picnic table. Since nobody had taken up residence on the outer wall by the window, I chose to sit down sideways at the picnic table, facing the center of the room with my back towards that unaccompanied wall. Not having any experience in my surroundings I did not want to chance being taken by surprise if I could at all avoid it. I also wanted to continue to take in my surroundings, unobtrusively.

So, I just sat there. A couple of times, I laid my head down, propped on my arms, so I could still see everything. But, there was no rest for me.

Waking Up To Consequences

My mind was relatively calm. Instead of my usual mental conversations, industriously composing plans A, B, C, D, and E, I had absolutely no plans at all. My spirit was so quiet, it was deafening to me. At one point, I went over and picked up the telephone to see if I could make a phone call, but the only numbers it would allow you to call were landlines and not cell phone numbers. The only landline numbers I could remember were to my mother and to my father. Everyone else had cell phones, so a landline did me no good at all. There was no way my dad could have come to get me. And, what would I possibly have to say to my mom?

"Oh yeah, you know that plane you are supposed to catch this afternoon? Well, I'm not sure if I will be able to pick you up from the airport, because I don't know if I will be out of jail in time."

I couldn't say that, so I just hung up the phone slowly, sat right back down on that cold metal picnic bench, and continued to listen.

What I heard, however, ensured I would not be sleeping.

By roughly four o'clock in the morning, most of the girls in the cells and on the floor were asleep, with the exception of two young college girls that came in together and looked as out of place as I did. They were both crying and cuddled up together in a corner, very nervous and completely out of sorts. There was another woman walking around that had, for some reason, taken her bra off and strapped it on top of her head. She walked around the cells and the common area, in circles, talking to herself. I had not seen my wrist

My Gift to God

mate since they unbuckled me from the wall to begin processing, which was fine with me. But, what made me more alert than anything else, while crouched on that metal picnic table, was the conversation between the two ladies who were located in the separate locked holding cells.

I could not see either one of them. I could only hear them. Because they were in separate holding areas, they were talking rather loud, with absolutely no concern if anyone else could be privy to their conversation. It went something like this:

"So, what are you in for this time?"

The response: "Well, I ain't sure yet."

"Why's that?"

The response: "Cause she's at the hospital and it depends on whether she dies or not, how long I stay in this time. Guess I'll be finding out in the morning. But, for now, I'm gonna shut my eyes awhile and sleep."

With that, the conversation ended and my spirit, once again, acknowledged choices I was consciously making.

Sitting there, I was surprised at how noiseless it was, with only the muffled cries of the two girls huddled in the corner and the one girl walking around mumbling under her breath. Accompanying this surprise, was the silence in my own mind. There was no panicking, nor were there any conversations, or deal makings and promises with God, going on inside my head.

I was not saying,

"God, if you will just get me out of this, I promise I will do this thing or I will never do this other thing ever again."

Not one single iota of that was registering inside.

My mind was quiet and subsequently, my spirit was also.

To this day, it amazes me how calm and still God made everything so I could capture every little detail of that night in my heart. I was not even correlating what I was experiencing that evening with what my dad had been through, so many years ago when being faced head on with his alcoholism and his drinking and driving. I had been so adamant that he face his own consequences, straighten up his life and fly right!

Talk about calling the kettle black. Well, here I sat, facing my own consequences, and I did not have a single person telling me I had to straighten up and get on course, or get with the program.

Not too long after the conversation acknowledging a possible murder indictment, I heard my last name called from the hallway, and I went to the door. There stood a different officer and she told me that I have a choice, to either wait until the bail hearing, sometime the next day, or someone was there to bail me out if I wanted to release my things to them. She then said,

"What are you doing in here, anyway? You don't look like you belong here."

My Gift to God

I was thinking, "Lady, you have no idea how much I agree with that statement, right now."

She then said she was going to do something she was not supposed to do and try to help me. The person picking me up had informed her he did not have enough money to bail me out. She wanted to know if there was enough cash in my belongings, or if I would want to write my PIN number on a piece of paper, since there was an ATM downstairs, so they could get the necessary money. I answered her question, signed a paper to release my belongings, and she told me to hang real close to the door, as she would be back promptly.

Off she went and another lady showed up with a tray full of Danishes and paper cups of water. She unlocked the cell door and, when she entered the common area, it was like chickens coming when you throw out scratch feed. Those ladies were flying from every nook and cranny to grab the food and head back to their respective areas.

As soon as they grabbed those hard Danishes off they went, back to their beds. It was nuts!

Chaos for two minutes, and then silence once again, with the exception of rattling papers, as the Danishes were opened.

I just stood there, taking it all in, until my friendly little officer came waddling back down the hallway, and said,

"Alright, little Missy, you are finally outta here."

Waking Up To Consequences

I was so thankful after signing my release papers, then taking the elevator back down to the loading dock and walking out a metal door, to see my friend Joe, leaned up against his jeep. He gave me a big hug and all of my belongings, stuffed in a bag. I wish that was the end of the story, but, actually, that was just the beginning for me. Going to collect my car from the impound lot as soon as they opened, I got home to change clothes just in time to head to work. When I walked in the house, I found my dad had fallen and hurt his leg in the shower that morning. All I could think was all the times everyone kept saying,

"What are you doing in here? You don't belong in here."

I was thinking to myself, "No, they were all correct. This is where I belonged, taking care of him, not locked up in a jail cell."

Still, here I was quietly taking it all in some more and reflecting on the mess I was making, but did not want anyone to know about.

I wanted it all to, simply, go quietly, away.

In fact, Joe had given me the name of an exceptional lawyer he knew would represent me well in court, and he told me to call him as soon as possible, after coming home from the hospital.

But, first, my mom was flying in that afternoon and I had too much to do to make up for lost time, so she would have no idea what had happened the night before. I decided I had to deal with one thing at a time. For now, surgery was on Monday, everything else would have to wait.

My Gift to God

Control, I had to regain control.

CHAPTER 15

Physical & Spiritual Recovery
《 —∞— 》

NO ONE KNEW OF MY incarceration, except for Joe and Sarai, and I chose to keep that under wrap completely, while spending the latter half of my weekend physically and mentally preparing for my surgery. Monday morning, I said my nervous goodbyes anxiously to Daddy, as he wrapped me lovingly up in his arms, calling me his baby, with kisses on my head. He attempted to calm me as I gave him final instructions that one of the neighbors would be by to tell him how the surgery had gone, then Momma and I drove to the hospital.

Pastor James and Wanda came to visit and pray with me before surgery, while Sarai came to sit with my mom, and then they took me back. One final conversation with my doctor, in which I reminded her,

"Remember, please do everything you can to keep everything intact." She reassured me and gave me her word that that was exactly what she intended to do, as long as everything looked clear of any suspicious tumors.

My Gift to God

With that, my anesthesia was administered, and I was out like a light.

The surgery was originally expected to last an hour and a half, and instead, it lasted over twice that long, making everyone a little anxious. The doctor explained all went well, although it was much more complicated than originally expected. To hold to the promise she had made to me, they had to leave two of the smaller tumors in, in order to maintain the integrity of my uterus, and not have to take it. My first question when becoming slightly coherent was,

"What did they have to do? Did they have to take it all?"

And I am certain, with a small grin towards her consternating daughter, my mother explained everything was still intact, inside of me, and it was now time to rest.

Rest did not come easy for me, however, as a person who always wanted to be three steps ahead and do a better than good job at every aspect of everything. Even in the midst of this surgery, I had set standards for my recovery. In my head, there were benchmarks that needed to be achieved, so I could say things were going well. One of the most poignant examples of this I can share with you is after that initial question to my mother and my passing back out, my next memory was being awakened by a nurse who had this contraption in her hands with a little ball inside of it. She was attempting to get me to blow in this little tube to make this ball go up in the air and all I could cognitively come up with in my brain was, "Why in the hell does this nurse want me to play this stupid game that looks like the breathalyzer I just did twice on Friday night?"

I tried to sit up in the bed and glared at her while demanding she leave and I did not appreciate that she was trying to make me play a game after surgery.

She tried to explain. I asked her, obnoxiously, again, to leave and as she was exiting the room, I emphatically told my mother, "I do not like her and do not want her to return." It was definitely not a graceful moment of delivery to this nurse, who was only trying to help me.

After the door closed, I looked at my mother, while attempting to sit up on the edge of the bed, and I said to her,

"Okay. Explain to me what it is that I have to do with that little ball, and why I have to do it, then I will figure out a way to get it done."

That is classic Sarah, right there!

Always in control, and will always find a way to get it done, once I know why I have to do it.

I could sum all of my thirty something years, up to that point in my life, with that one, simple statement.

My mother explained why it was necessary, the nurse came back in, I apologized, and I did exactly what she asked, before she resolutely pushed my morphine pump and out I went again to rest. I am certain, they were ready for a cessation to my shenanigans. The rest of my days in the hospital went pretty much along those same lines.

They told me I needed to walk the halls and I would push myself to walk further than they wanted, just to prove I could, and then I would pay for it.

Resting was not on my radar. Recuperating, regaining control, and getting back to my normal was what I had in my sights.

I had no realistic concept of what was on the horizon for this recovery time.

The two to three days I would spend in the hospital I heard the doctor tell me, two months prior, turned into a week due to the extensive nature of the surgery. The two to three weeks out of work I also chose to hear in her office, resulted in fourteen weeks for the very same reason.

My abilities to rehabilitate quicker had nothing to do with my mind and what I could accomplish. But, God, He was attempting to procure an altogether different scope of recovery for me.

His plan was not just a physical recovery, but the accompaniment of a spiritual recovery that I was not ready for. Or was I?

The old saying goes, hind sight is twenty/twenty. Well, it really is! Looking back on that time, I can see, unequivocally,

His hand in grabbing my attention.

His hand in making me still.

His hand in saying, "I have pursued you for so very long. Now it is time to rip open your heart and show you the truth."

Recovery.

Physically and Spiritually combined.

Today, I thank God, He, literally, sat me on my haunches, where I could not even walk down the hall and running was not an option on the table any longer, either.

There I sat, still before Him, and He was about to reveal to me things I did not even know I wanted or needed to see.

Even prior to my surgery, His work was evident, as I had not made any plans for anyone other than my mother to take care of me. In my naivety, I really did think my recovery would be a piece of cake. Luckily, I have wonderful friends who know my personality and how I think I can do everything myself, but they knew I would need as much help as possible. The way things just worked out also showed God's hand in the planning. Without any communication with each other, this was what happened.

My mother flew in for surgery on Saturday afternoon and stayed until the following Saturday morning.

One of my best friends, Caritas, flew in from Alabama, the Friday evening that I arrived home from the hospital, and was able to take my mother to the airport the next morning.

Caritas stayed until the following Friday, when she, literally, met Adam at the airport with the keys to my car. His flight arrived, an

My Gift to God

hour prior to her departure, and they had arranged to meet in the terminal at the airport. Not only did she deliver the keys to him, but also some pertinent advice. She instructed him to make me let him take care of me, because she knew I would try to do it all myself. She had also given me a swift kick in the rear end before she left, explaining to me I needed to allow him to take care of me, instead of acting like I was a superwoman when I could not even get out of bed or off of the couch without assistance, much less do anything else on my own.

Adam stayed a week and flew out the following Friday. His flight left within an hour of my good friend, Amy, arriving from Tennessee, and she stayed until Adam's mother drove out for two weeks and took Amy to the airport.

None of this was orchestrated by them or me.

It all, just happened!

The coordination of the times was also amazing because I could not drive for two reasons. First, my license had been suspended, upon my arrest, but also because I could not physically drive for twelve weeks, due to the doctors strict orders.

God's grace and mercy was even evident during this time, as well. All of my restrictions from the arrest coincided with the time I was off from work. I had received a letter from the State of Missouri, informing me my license was suspended for twelve weeks, and that was the time I could not drive, anyway. While Adam was there caring for me, I told him everything that had taken place the weekend prior to surgery. Although I expected sheer disappointment from him, he supported me and could see the changes taking place already. That week, I contacted the lawyer that Joe had recommended, and Adam drove down to meet him, give him all of the information, paperwork and my payment. My court date was the week after I was released to drive. When I went to court, the charges were reduced to only a city citation and no charges filed against me. I was, however, required to do community service, drive on a restricted license for three more months, which was home and work only, to attend a drug and alcohol class, alcohol counseling and MADD (Mothers Against Drunk Driving) meeting.

I immediately signed up for my community service and when I walked in the lady looked at me and guess what she said?

"What are you doing here? You don't belong here."

I thought to myself, "Here we go, again."

She then began going through her files of possibilities for my community service, looked at a paper on her desk and said,

"Aw, yes this is the one for you. A thrift store that supports a battered women's shelter."

The store was merely ten minutes from my house and the cleanest thrift store I had ever walked the aisles of. The people were exceptionally kind, also. Twenty hours of service was the requirement, within six months, and this location let you work at your own pace, when you had time. Diligently, I worked mine off in less than two months, spending the Christmas season there, and enjoyed the work and the people.

God was bringing me down, notch by notch, opening my eyes to servanthood.

Adam had made the decision to come back out for the winter season and had told me, while I was still in the hospital, that he no longer had any questions about us. He knew he was supposed to be there with me. During his week of caring for me, he had also secured his previous position. And after returning to Tennessee, he began making preparations to come out, once again, to Kansas City for the winter season.

After his mother had returned to Tennessee, I had two weeks at the house with just my dad and me, still unable to drive legally or physically. Felicia, Adam's mom, had made sure I had everything I needed, prior to her departure, and this time was really mind opening to me. Adam drove out the third week of October and humbly, without complaint, continued to take care of me. When my community service began, he drove me to the thrift store and picked me up several hours later. He also drove me to my alcohol counseling, which was interesting because the counselor mainly wanted to discuss my dad's alcoholism and the effect it had on my adult decision making. After a lengthy discussion, she signed off on my paperwork and cleared me of the need for any further counseling.

Things were ticking along progressively, and then came a Saturday meeting in which I, along with other alcohol offenders, met for three hours in the basement of an old run down business complex, in an area of town I had never been in before. Walking down a rusty metal staircase, I was met at the bottom by a gentleman, sitting at a table, filling out some paperwork. He sat there for a few minutes before acknowledging my presence, then, slowly, he raised his eyes up, peering over his bifocals at me, and then tilted his head slightly to the left, to look around me, and said curiously,

"Are you here for the meeting?" I replied, "Yes, sir. I am."

He sat back in his chair, took his glasses off, and said, "Well. Explain to me what in the world are you here for? I can already tell, you do not belong in this meeting!"

He was emphatic that, for the love of mankind, he wished he could just sign me out and let me be on my way. Inside, my mind was whirling as to how many times it was possible to repeatedly hear the same statement reiterated.

But, today, I am glad I attended that meeting because, as I took my seat in the back corner of the room, where I could watch all that was going on around me, my eyes were once again opened. All of these people did not understand why I was where I was, but, God, knew exactly what I needed to see and hear each step along the way.

My Gift to God

The reality of the night I spent in jail was just one layer of the onion, and this meeting was about to tear that onion wide open to shed light on how much I had been spared from, most of my life and even over these last few months. The evidence of God's hand and His grace and mercy was so externally brought to light that morning, I would be unable to deny it.

After everyone arrived and were in their seats, this guy showed he clearly meant to get down to business. An older, grey haired gentleman, an ex-cop and now a counselor, began to explain to all of us why he led these sessions. It was to level with people about their realities.

He began by asking various questions about what we had each been arrested for. The answers were all alcohol related, mainly driving but also public intoxication, among other things. Then he began asking about our lives and how we grew up, along with what our present family situations looked like.

The answers, blew me away.

There were so many who did not know their fathers or had poor relationships, if any relationship at all, with them. He began bridging the gap between why the drinking and the impact from our relationships with our family. I witnessed two guys, who were, admittedly, members of the same gang, both brought close to tears in this discussion. They opened up to talk about being raised by grandmothers, with no male figure around at all, much less really knowing who their fathers were. As for their mothers, one was a prostitute and the other was in prison. Then a female prostitute spoke up about trying to survive with no family around. Her daughter was there in the same room. She was also a prostitute.

I could not even move, anchored to my seat, as I listened to these stories, while this guy just stood up there and let people open up. There was no judgment, all he was doing was bringing reality to light, or shedding light on the darkness in our lives.

It was astounding at how open everyone was.

After he had most of us on an emotional roller coaster, he began talking about our present situations. How much money we had spent and the amount of time spent in jail, away from our own families. Now remember, I was in the very back corner of the room and he started on the opposite side of the room, opposite corner. One by one, he had us answer what it had cost us in time and financially. He wrote each answer on a large whiteboard that extended the full length, front of the room. When the first person answered, they said, "Five thousand dollars and two days." I thought that was a little excessive. But, as the answers kept flowing, there were several people answering ten thousand dollars and three or four days, with one repeat offender even giving figures of twelve thousand and ten days. By the time he got to my corner, I was feeling pretty uncomfortable because I knew, financially, I was in a much better

My Gift to God

position than a lot of the people in the room. I kept recalculating in my head, I must have missed something.

The closer he came to me, the faster I kept adding up attorney, court costs, money to the state, insurance adjustment, counseling costs, the fee for community service placement.

Over and over again, adding up in my head and when he was less than five people away, I looked anxiously on the board, searching for the lowest cost and lowest amount of time spent. What I saw was five thousand dollars and two days, the first answer given. When he finally reached me, I sat there for a minute, fidgeting in my chair, then delivered my answer,

"One thousand five hundred dollars and eight hours in jail."

Quickly, everyone turned to stare at me in disbelief. The instructor replied skeptically, "Does that include court costs and attorney fees?" When I affirmed, unobtrusively, that the figure, indeed, included everything, he then said,

"I told you, you didn't belong in here! You must have had a great lawyer and someone else on your side because I have never heard those numbers that low."

But, I was exactly where I needed to be. Exactly where God needed me to be!

No one else could believe it either. There were a couple of comments about the pretty little white girl having favor thrown her way, but he immediately redirected things back to the board. The total cost and time away from our families added up to over $350,000 and over 200 hundred days in jail.

He then advised us all to remember what the drinks we had consumed that day had cost us.

Nervous laughter filled the room, followed by silence as he just stared at us, blankly, letting it sink in. He then asked us to think about what the true cost for that day had been, and after a moment of complete silence, he dismissed the class and told us he hoped to never see us again. I agreed wholeheartedly with that statement.

Attempting to exit the room as quick as possible, I could not wait to get in the car with Adam, to share with him what had happened. Instead, when I got in the car I could only sit in silence, with my spirit crying inside for the people I had just shared four hours with, and for the realization of the mess I had caused, yet had been spared so much more than I deserved.

God was still pursuing me, but it was no longer a chase.

For the first time, since I was nine-years-old, I no longer wished to run, but just to sit in awe of all that was happening, in my midst, with no doing of my own.

Not long after that counseling meeting, I spent another Saturday afternoon with a group called MADD (Mothers Against Drunk Driving). Captivated, I listened to a mother recount the story of her son's death, accompanied by pictures on a screen, in a darkened room. With no sound, other than her voice, slow and soft, still emotional after the many years that had passed since his accident, the only other noise were the gentle cries of those in the room listening.

One more acknowledgment of choices, and the bearing on other's lives.

The courts knew what they were doing when they sentenced some people to these sessions. As someone who is an observer, and who takes things in quietly, it affected me deeply then, and still affect me today. I can still see that room, with the figures on the board and the pictures of the car where that mothers son passed away, as vivid as I see my husband standing at the end of the garden path on our wedding day.

These moments are imprinted deep within me, residing in a place untouched by the world, because they were given to me from my Maker, never to be forgotten.

He really was silencing my mind for a while, and taking away the distractions I had surrounded myself with, only because I chose to listen to Him.

In fact, prior to my journey of court, counseling, and community service, when I was still at home, barely able to walk from room to room, He had begun gravitating my attention towards Him. Those days were filled with much boredom. After waking each day and making my way, ever so slowly, down the stairs from my bedroom to the living area, I had three stations set up that consumed my days.

A reading chair with an ottoman, in the corner by the window, so I could see outside and read.

A bar stool by the kitchen island, where I ate, played games on the computer, put jigsaw puzzles together, or surfed the Internet.

Then the couch, for sleeping or watching television.

Those were my three stations throughout the day until evening, when I would make a slow, climb, up the stairs, to return to bed. The stairs exhausted me, so I stayed on the main level during the day, moving from one station to the other; reading in the chair, eating at the counter, playing on my computer and then retiring to the couch. Get up, recycle, and repeat, although even getting up from the couch or chair was a challenge the first several weeks. Once I got past sleeping most of my days away, I began spending more time in my reading chair. Although a friend from work had given me some books to read, I felt drawn to open my bible. I did this for a couple of days, just kind of ruffling through the pages, and it felt more like I was playing bible book bingo than actually reading it. I realized that, although I grew up in church and had been in and out of church over the years that I had never really sat down and just read it.

It was more a book on the shelf, or a book that stayed in my car, to be carried into church on the Sundays I would attend a service. But, other than knowing it was the word of God, and it contained stories of people, it really had no influence on me.

My Gift to God

It was weird to acknowledge that to myself. It was just a symbol of a religion I really knew nothing about.

This began leading to some questions. What is Christianity, really? And, what do I know about it?

I came up empty handed.

Nothing.

So, I put the book back down.

The next day I picked it up again. As I flipped through the pages, I stopped at the list of the books of the Bible, and just stared at it, intimidated. Remembering that Amy, several years ago, had given me a small pamphlet on how to read the Bible in a year, I began flipping through the various items tucked in the pages. I pulled the pamphlet out, inspecting its directives of dividing out several books and chapters for daily reading, and then decided I would grab some paper clips on my way downstairs the following day and divide the book into readable sections. Once again, I laid the book back down and carried on with the rest of my day, without much thought.

But, something happened that afternoon when I returned to my reading chair, for my afternoon sequence of daily rotations. I sat there, staring out the window, and heard this still small voice in my spirit tell me,

"Do not initiate anything."

This particular day, Caritas, my caretaker for the week, was gone to the store and I sat there, thinking,

"What? What the heck does that mean?"

But, I heard it crystal clear and I knew, just as I knew when He had spoken to me that Adam was my husband, and that my dad was okay when I was a child, that this was God speaking to my heart.

He spoke those same words, over and over again into my heart, in a very simple, slow, soft directive. As the weeks tarried on; I came to understand why. Because He knew in my boredom, after everyone had left, I would try and fill my time, but He desired I would fill my time with Him, and His word, instead.

This was not clear when I first heard it, but, as time perpetually ticked on, the relevancy of those gentle words became apparent. After dividing the Bible into an attainable approach of accomplishing the task of reading this book, I decided the next day I would begin reading it.

One day at a time, sweet Jesus.

What I did not anticipate, however, was, although I started trying to read these divided out sections, God had another plan. Each day, during my reading chair rotation, I would finger through and read some things, here and there, all the while with that still, small voice inside reminding me not to initiate anything.

Here was the test.

Did I listen to that voice that had some wonderment to it?

My Gift to God

Or, did I choose to flip through my phone and fill up my days with other things? That would have been the easy choice, but something was changing inside of me, a curiosity was becoming ignited.

The first day, alone, left to my own devices, slowly, carefully, I inched my way down the stairs to fix myself some oatmeal for breakfast. Daddy came up to check in on me and then I sat at the kitchen island for a little while, staring at my reading chair. However, a new station had been added to my daily rotation, to help rebuild my strength to walk again, the sidewalk outside of my house. Twice daily, I would walk short distances. First, to the end of the driveway, then slowly as the days and weeks passed, I would add another driveway down the sidewalk. Until, many weeks later, I could make it down the road to the stop sign. After a month of practice, the entire block eventually became my track. But, this particular day, I only planned to walk two driveways down from my house. On my way out of the house, after staring at my reading chair, I gathered my bible and set it on the front porch for when I returned from my not too distant, although a ten minute, walk. I returned to sit on the stoop of my front porch, and opened this book, a birthday gift from my mother back when I was dating Stacey, bound in blue leather with my name printed on the front in pretty silver italic letters. I began reading, in Genesis, chapter one.

I sat there that morning and read halfway through Genesis before deciding to go inside. With much determination, I climbed the stairs slowly, went into my office and gathered a pink pen before returning back downstairs to start in Genesis, chapter one, once again. Something switched that day, and I was beginning to put sermons I had heard over the years to test with the scripture. And, although some questions began piling up, there was an urgency to read more. Over the next few days, I picked up no other books beside my reading chair, just this one, blue, leather bound book.

This book, called the Bible.

Up until then, that was all it had really been, a book. Although I had carried it to church over the past ten years or so, the silver lined pages were still perfectly intact, containing no tears or ruffled pages. Simply another book on the shelf, brought down when it was convenient, or sat in my car collecting dust.

But, now, it was coming alive.

The words and promises inside, and the stories began making some sort of sense to me. Again, I would hear those four little words, do not initiate anything.

And, there became nothing to initiate, really, as my free time was spent with such a fervency to read and to understand.

I wanted it! I desired it!

For the first time in my life, that blue book became the Word of God to me. The games on the computer and the shows on the television could no longer hold my attention, and my days became filled with reading, studying, and using my little pink pen. As I physically became stronger, I walked a little longer and then sat on the front stoop of my house, sometimes until evening, for the fresh air in my lungs and the fresh air in my spirit.

As my rotations in the house dwindled, and I was able to drive a very short distance, with a pillow across my lap to brace the seat belt, I would take my Bible and drive one mile to a pretty little park close to my house. Although my driving restrictions had not been lifted, either by my doctor or the state, I still pushed the boundaries, just a hair. The park was home to refurbished old houses and a church with a pretty butterfly and herbal garden with wooden hewn benches. A water wheel house, complete with a working waterwheel, sat beside an old mercantile general store. Throughout the buildings and property were many serene trails that wound around the park, and a field full of buffalo. I began taking my daily walks there, as my strength increased and I read, still with a fervency, internally, to learn more.

Until one day, I landed, in the book of Ruth.

This was a pivotal moment in my relationship with God and His word.

I began reading through the book of Ruth, and then reread it again.

Physical & Spiritual Recovery

Flipping back through the pages, anger began to overtake me. I was searching for the truth.

All of the years I had justified my feelings for women, basing them on scriptures that most lesbians would use to retort the infallibility of our relationships and our feelings, and I could not find it! I had based so many things on this one section of verses, but never had I taken the time to read the entire book for myself and understand it, in context.

But, this day here it was, straight in my face.

Those verses did not and could not support homosexuality, yet I had stood on them as truth without ever checking it out fully for myself.

I had taken the words of others and used them as my own.

I had made a stand, raised my rainbow banner proudly, and this day, I realized the deception. I was so utterly angry, in the depths of my soul that I wanted to toss my pretty, blue Bible into the water by that wheelhouse!

Why?

Why!

Why had God allowed me to believe these things? Why had He allowed His own words to be manipulated into some false sense of security because of two little verses?

Wailing up inside of me, I shouted at God verbally and shook my fist in anger, so reproved with my pride being destroyed!

My Gift to God

I thought of all the Pride marches I had attended, donning my rainbow-touted clothing, marching in the streets and parks of Atlanta and various other cities. Defiantly arguing with street preachers about the word of God, all the while holding my girlfriend's hand or kissing her right in front of them in defiance.

What had I done and why had God allowed me to do it?!

The questions were seemingly endless, as I drove back home. I threw that book on my reading chair and left it there for three days while I sulked and mouthed off to God in every expletive known. I decided if He could allow me to believe things not of Him then He could certainly handle my emotions. If He couldn't, and hell fire flew down from heaven on me, then, He wasn't the God I thought He was, anyway!

And, do you know what He did?

Nothing.

He did absolutely, nothing but speak, once again, to my heart to not initiate anything!

But, boy, did I want to!

I wanted to call up any number of my friends, and have them come get me out of that house to go drink. But, I was too tired, and instead, I slept. After the third day of this anger continuing to rise inside of me, I decided it was time to find the truth, so back into the Bible I went.

Although there was some audaciousness to my attitude, He had placed a hunger so deep within me I was not going to give up. I wanted the truth, and I wanted to find it myself, not from sermons I had listened to or people I had heard discuss their beliefs.

I wanted God's truth myself, and I wanted it in black and white.

Nothing else could satiate my soul until I knew.

This was God's plan all along, to reveal lies I had believed, and to begin to untangle the deception that had surrounded my heart.

No one else could reach me. Only He could, in His way and in His time.

As the weeks passed, the journey continued, even after Adam came back to Kansas City. I would not even ask Adam the questions that were building in my mind. Only God could write the answers to those questions on my heart and in my life.

With God setting me still, with no way to escape, I became His again. But no longer was He after a temporary relationship.

He was coming for His daughter.

CHAPTER 16

Coming Out of the Closet Backwards

« —∞— »

WHEN ADAM ARRIVED BACK TO Kansas City, he knew he was encountering a different Sarah than the girl he left in the springtime. This was the girl who was a closer glimpse of the one he fell in love with many years ago as he clandestinely watched a slow transformation begin to unfold before him.

Not only did he witness the questions in my eyes, but, also, the running shoes being slowly put away.

Returning to the closet what belonged in the closet had nothing to do with my sexuality. Instead, what was coming out of the closet was this girl being led by her father to meet her mate. But, coming out of my gay closet backwards was no easy walk down the street. Physically, my strength was returning, with each addition of a walk past an added driveway, which eventually turned into walking around the block and then walking around the block multiple times in a day. Although slowing down was substantially more difficult than I expected, the rest on my body and on my spiritual heart had been good. Then the realization set in. I would need to return to normal living, away from the confines of my neighborhood, back to work, and back to friends.

No one but Adam was aware of my legal restrictions. My tiredness made for a good excuse for a while, but then the interrogations launched incessantly. The holidays were just around the corner. Celebrations I normally, not only attended, but, occasionally, had hosted were in the makings. My absence was noted, and people were raising their eyebrows. Who was this girl, now, and what was happening to Sarah?

Content to go to work and then go directly home, although my required community service and meetings played into that some, my desires began changing. I wanted to be home, and not out partying and drinking until the sun came up. No longer did I desire progressive dinners starting at one restaurant or bar for drinks and appetizers before moving on to a second, third, or sometimes even a fourth location before passing out or driving home. My heart was settling into a newfound comfort, where I felt safe and I felt loved.

Internally, I was still healing from the trauma to my uterine cavity and the doctor had informed me this would take close to a year. But, more importantly, my heart was also beginning to heal.

Adam's return that winter cemented our relationship into one that was not conjugal at all, but rather a deep emotional state that resonated into our hearts becoming one. Pastor James began counseling both Adam and I, separately, and he knew Adam's intentions, with this stay in Kansas City, were to "Come and get me." Adam had shared that with me upon arriving in mid-October.

He conveyed, clearly, there was nothing in the city for him, except for me and that he came to get me and, well, get me, he did.

He, really, had always had me. I had just been unwilling to give in, and unwilling to listen to that voice in my heart.

He was the one on this earth, who had always known me; the one God had created for me, and had created me for him.

He was, and still is, the one who has never once taken my past and perverted it or taken it out of context.

Never. Not Once.

He has respected parts of me that did not deserve respect, and has shown me what a true God-given love really is. I realized there was no question any longer about our relationship. Although I still had some independence issues to work out, God was already dealing with that, as well.

That following February, I received a call from my mother that my Pappaw had passed away. I made immediate arrangements to fly home to Tennessee, attend the funeral and to stay a couple of extra days with Adam's mom. It was on this trip, I made some impactful decisions regarding our future together.

I was tired of being so far away from my family, I missed the mountains, and I just missed home. While staying with Felicia, after the funeral, I began asking God some questions about perception and the impact of my decisions. Each of those three Tennessee mornings, I woke up, had my coffee, and then drove over to Adam's place, although he was still in Kansas City, to just sit.

I would venture out on his back deck or walk through the field, and simply sit and think. This is what I knew:

I knew if I went back to KC and said, "Okay, Adam, we will do it your way, and I will come back to Tennessee", my life would change, dramatically.

I would be letting go of a lot of things. And, when I say things, I mean "things!"

I would be moving from an enormous home, with a three-car garage, to a one thousand square foot, singlewide trailer, on five acres.

I would be giving up my upcoming promotion and another move to either Savannah, Georgia or Boise, Idaho.

I would be letting go of all perceptions by everyone else to become his wife. No longer would I be considered a self-sustaining, single woman, making all of the decision for myself, and for my dad, alone.

I would be saying yes to a marriage I felt was ordained by God, and saying no to my past life.

And, I really was not sure if I could come out of that closet backwards enough, to be good enough. But, I was willing to try, after sitting there for three days and talking it out with God.

I was being real with Him about my fears, and about my hesitations, and asking for His help in saying yes, to my future husband.

I did not share this with anyone. In fact, upon returning to Kansas City, I did not broach the subject with Adam for one whole week. I knew I had to be sure I would not go back on my word, and I understood flippant decisions were no longer acceptable, because now I knew the truth. I had read the Bible, front to back. I had fought and cried and yelled and screamed, until truth was revealed, and had been written on my heart. It was no longer about the church, or a preacher, or my family. It was me, and it was God. Now, it was time to give everything I had to Him.

It was at this point I had to learn to trust in Him fully and I felt I really had nothing to lose by trusting Him. For all of my life, my decisions, without His input, had come up completely fruitless and tangled into messy vines.

No longer could I offer up lip service to trusting Him, I had to come to this place within myself that was willing to resolutely surrender it all, including my independence, and my carefully crafted contingency plans, and rely solely on trust. This does not mean that the spirit of independence that He created me with would evaporate,

My Gift to God

but rather my independence could be used for good, instead of self-deprecation and self-absorption.

It is difficult to put to words all that was happening inside of me, so quickly. But, just as God had taken me to Kansas City, he was now bringing me home, by way of Adam McKinnis.

You should have seen the sparkle in Adam's eyes when I told him I was ready. He asked quizzically,

"Ready? For what?" I told him with these exact words,

"I have thought and fought and prayed about it until I can no more, and I am ready to do things your way. I am ready to go home. And, I am ready to be your wife."

It was the end of March, and the whirlwind of excitement began.

The question was how were we going to get thirty five hundred square feet of stuff into a one thousand square foot trailer, it was hysterical. He hauled part of the stuff on his drive back and then built a cabin for my dad, on his property, before we returned the third week in April. I began going through that house, like the Tasmanian devil, giving away things, and throwing things out by the truckload. I have no idea how many trucks from different community organizations came and filled up to the brim with belongings.

The expensive items, like my baby grand piano were listed for sale and the items all sold relatively quickly. It was a constant revolving door of people picking up items, Adam leaving with a trailer full and then the day my dad and I were set to leave, more people arriving I just gave stuff away to. We managed to fit all we possibly could into the largest U-Haul truck I could find, and a friend from Tennessee flew in to KC to drive it back, while I loaded my car down with two dogs a cat, and my dad, before departing for a memorable drive home.

It was difficult walking away from that house into the unknown, but looking forward to my future with Adam, was worth it all.

That drive with my daddy took two days, as we decided to take our time. It was a good thing we did, because I had no more put the car in reverse to back out of the driveway, when both dogs puked in the backseat. I was so frustrated, and did not want to have to walk back into that house, but I found some paper towels in the garage and tried to clean it up best I could. Thankfully, I brought the roll with us because five more times over the course of the first two hours of our trip, it happened, again. Pulling over on the side of the interstate, mad at first, we decided to make the best of the situation. All we could really do was laugh, anyway. Away we went, after the final incident, with the windows rolled down and the fresh, cool, April air blowing in our faces, as we traveled on.

We listened to Daddy's CD collection of Waylon Jennings and Willie Nelson all the way across Missouri, passing by the Arches in St. Louis, that Laurie and I had traveled past four years earlier, headed in the opposite direction. We got off I-70 and decided to take country roads through Illinois, and on down into Kentucky, before stopping for the night. The next morning, we continued on into Tennessee, through Nashville, and then on to Adam's. The look of surprise and happiness on my Daddy's face when He saw he had his own little cabin, right beside the trailer, was worth the smell of puke and driving all the way from Kansas City with the windows down!

Adam did an amazing job with this little one room custom cabin complete with kitchen, bed and bathroom. Handmade burlap curtains were on the windows, a desk for his computer, bookshelves with his books and a television and radio.

He was set up, and it was perfect!

As daddy stepped onto the front porch, complete with a rocking chair, with a glimmer in his eye, he said,

"Now! Good! Good!" Which in daddy-speak, meant nothing could be better!

Watching my dad and Adam interact with each other and witnessing the forethought Adam had used in preparing a home for him, only deepened my respect for Adam. He was experiencing as much change as we were and was inviting us both, unselfishly, into his life, home and family. In that instant, he portrayed how much he truly cared about both of us and that he understood the significance and responsibility of caring for my dad, as a component of who I was, as his daughter. Although I had not always done the best job possible in caring for my dad, Adam was now choosing to shoulder that responsibility with me, and it warmed me from the inside out.

Unable to verbally express my thoughts and emotions, I simply took his hand in mine, looked him straight in the eye, and whispered sincerely, "Thank You!"

With one week off from work before starting at my new location, I unpacked, re-arranged, and cleaned. Poor Adam had no idea what had happened when all of this stuff entered his bachelor pad, but his mom was ecstatic. She said, for the first time, ever, it had been made to look like a home. I just laughed and the following week, I started back to work. But Adam and I were also working on a secret.

We had not enlightened our family that we planned to be married the end of May. We wanted the wedding to be a small, intimate moment, surrounded with very specific people. We also knew the more time we gave our mothers to prepare, the more out of hand it would become. Slyly, we began making arrangements and on Mother's Day I asked mine and Adam's mom if I could take them both to lunch. After picking them both up, we started the thirty-mile trek down the interstate as I informed them I needed to make a quick stop first, before heading to the restaurant. We pulled into a parking lot and while they were chit chatting away, I pulled a bag from the back and sheepishly said,

"I brought ya'll some snacks, because it is going to be a little while before we get to the restaurant."

They both stared at me, very confused, as I pointed out the window to one of the stores in front of us, and explained,

My Gift to God

"Because, we are going inside there."

They said, "The Verizon store?" and I said, "No, the one next door."

Dumbfounded, they just looked at me with these tiny smiles inching across their faces, as they looked at the bridal store sign. Simultaneously, they both squealed,

"What?! In there? Are ya'll getting married?"

The cat was out of the bag. They hurriedly opened their doors, laughing and giggling like two schoolgirls, as the inquisition of when, where, and how long had we known began. I told them three weeks from that day, at my aunt and uncle's property, in the same spot where Adam and I had sat in the grass by the creek bank that day right before my Mammaw passed away. I had already asked my Aunt and she had agreed, and now it was time to find a dress. After I picked out several dresses to try on and came out of the dressing room wearing the first one, they were nowhere to be found.

Still like schoolgirls, I could hear their cackles across the store, as they were eagerly looking for their own dresses to wear.

Excitement! The day was approaching!

CHAPTER 17

God's Promises Fulfilled
《 —∞— 》

TUCKED AWAY IN THE BACKROOM of the bridal shop was the bridal gown I had envisioned, the intricate details of my dream brought to fruition. Floor length, with a tiny chapel train, the stunning, elegant, sleeveless dress was covered in cream lace, accompanied by a trailing full-length veil. The completion of our garden wedding was coming together perfectly, exactly as we had pictured. As the day approached, devoted friends were making travel plans from Indianapolis, Alabama, Nashville, and Kansas City, even on such brief notice. Pastor James was flying in to perform our ceremony, as he said he would not miss it for the world. Avery, who had introduced Adam and me, used his artist's eye to create a stunning ring set that was Adam's vision come to life. Cast out of family gold with a beautiful emerald stone surrounded by Gaelic etchings, the McKinnis family crest motto is inscribed, "Gift of God and King." As Adam slipped it slowly on my ring finger while speaking our vows, it was my first look at this beautiful creation.

It was the most perfect, magical day.

My Gift to God

The three weeks leading up to our wedding were hectic, but calm, all at the same time. The rentals for the tables, chairs, dishes, silver and glassware was only one phone call away, as well as the photographer and caterer. My cousin, Melissa, who has an eye for exceptionally beautiful details, took the vision in my mind and transformed the tree-filled yard into a magical wooded fairy tale, along the creek. Tables, covered with handpicked, varied fabrics, were topped with wine bottles converted into water, tea, and lemonade carafes, and adorned by metal signs of prayer and faith. China and crystal were placed alongside silverware, wrapped in rosemary sprigs from our property. Hanging lights and multi-colored candle holders were strung under the old pine trees, adorned with some of my paintings, while pictures of Adam and I, in our younger years, had been placed on lines with clothes pins for everyone else's laughter and enjoyment.

Felicia had created our scrumptious cake and cupcakes, while also assisting the caterer with steak and chicken kabobs for our dinner reception. My mom helped me position white chairs, for our guests, in a circle, in a grassy knoll beside the creek, with only a small entranceway. Fresh flower petals were strewn across the path. Beautiful blue, green, and white hydrangeas adorned the ground and waist-high columns at the site chosen for our intimate ceremony.

God's Promises Fulfilled

There was no rehearsal, just some last minute planning, before I headed to stay at our honeymoon location one night early, in the Captain's Quarters on The Delta Queen Riverboat, which is a steamboat on the Tennessee River. I had invited my lovely friend, Kristie, to join me that evening, and we sat out on the deck in rocking chairs until nearly midnight, enjoying the cool breeze from the river, talking and laughing, before retiring to the room to sleep. However, around 4:00 I realized there would be no sleeping for me.

I felt a pressing on my heart to write a letter to Adam, to be given to him prior to our taking vows. I quietly got up, went down to the steward and asked if he had a pen and paper. He provided some stationary and then brought some freshly brewed coffee to me on the deck.

This was a pivotal morning, as well as a pivotal day, for Adam and me.

This day was a fulfillment of promises God had spoken to my heart, nearly a decade prior.

This was a fulfillment of prophecy that both Adam and I had received, together and separately, and I remembered the man who had been in the parking lot of the bar, so many years ago, who had asked me,

"Where is your husband, Adam?"

And, now, I knew.

My Gift to God

Adam was about to meet me at the circular alter, surrounded by one hundred of our closest friends and family. But, while resting in what would be our honeymoon suite, the urging to speak from my heart to Adam prior to our wedding was consuming and consistent. The best way to communicate with him, since we had not spoken to each other in a day, was through this letter.

This letter, represented all of the promises I was about to make to my husband when we spoke those vows before God and those witnesses. This was not a lighthearted exchange, this was fulfillment, and I knew it in the depths of my soul. In that letter, I expressed I could not take my vows until, first, I made him some promises.

Those promises were scriptural and I understood by making a vow with him in front of God, I was submitting to him as head of our home. Now, some people get so bent out of shape over that scripture and think it is demeaning to women, but it is quite the opposite. Because, just as it instructs women to submit to their husbands, it also instructs the men to love their wives as Christ loved the church. This is such a beautiful representation of the marriage union because Christ loves and respects the church and longs for the church to draw closer. And, when respect is delivered by the wife, setting the husband as head of the home, they transform the union into one where each person is drawing closer to the other through respect, adoration and, most importantly, a humble nature by both the husband and wife. A woman desires to be adored and wanted and a man desires respect and longing. What better way to deliver this, than through both, mutually, humbling themselves to each other?

It is cyclical, reverent, and all-encompassing, this marriage union I was entering into.

By knowing how much respect, care, and concern my Adam had shown me, and I was not even yet his wife, I knew it would only increase. There were no illusions of a perfect marriage, but I knew we were made for each other, by, God, and the design of the marriage union that God himself ordained, is what I desired.

There would be no fakeness in this marriage.

We were not only in love with each other, but we were, and still are best friends. And although neither of us is perfect, we are perfect for each other. This morning of our wedding, I knew he needed to hear, in my words, what that day meant to me.

No more flippant relationships or decisions.

This was until death do us part, and I wanted it no other way.

The more I wrote, the more at peace I was. After writing, I went and laid down quietly for several more hours. That morning Kristie and I had breakfast before we went our separate ways. I drove to a local fresh market and waited on their doors to open, so I could pick the beautiful hydrangeas for my wedding bouquet and add them to the purple thistles that had been gathered from the side of the road.

My Gift to God

The thistles were, in fact, another representation of our life. Back so many years ago, when he had prepared that birthday meal for me, I had stopped and cut some on the way to his house. They were something we both enjoyed with their prickly leaves and bold, beautiful flowers, but most of all because of their Irish/Scottish semblance that represented both of our heritages. Upon returning to My Aunt Carla's, we wrapped the stems with ribbon and some pretty pins, and made a boutonniere for my daddy and Adam out of the thistles. After tidying up as many details as I could, Melissa assured me they had it all under control. I walked to my Cousin Leigh Anne's house, which was just over a little wooden bridge that crossed the creek to her Georgian style home, to rest before going to have my hair done.

Sitting in the chair, at my good friend Jody's home, who was also my hairdresser, we talked the entire time about where God had brought us from. She had been taking care of my hair for close to seventeen years now, and in fact, had been the same person to fix my hair the morning I married Dawson, so many years ago. She had also seen me through my silent years, with Stacey dictating my hairstyle, to my wild and crazy days before going to Kansas City, and then coming home. Here I was, in her chair, once again.

She said this was the calmest and most at peace she had ever seen me and the twinkle in my eyes told her all she needed to know.

This was the day the Lord had ordained.

God's Promises Fulfilled

She could not have been more correct. Upon returning to my cousin's home, I went to the upstairs window and looked over the ceremony spot in the woods, past the barn, and I could see so much bustling activity. Leigh Anne's husband, Virgil, was already directing traffic. I caught a glimpse of my Adam, driving down the long driveway with my daddy, and my heart was anxious to see him. I had arranged for a box to be delivered to him upon his arrival, to be opened alone, which held two pipes. One for my daddy, and the other was for Adam, to replace the Savinelli Churchill pipe that had been broken so many years ago, when he had thrown it after realizing who he had thought was to be his wife, was pushing him away.

But, on this day it was delivered with a note hoping this one would never endure a break of that kind, and accompanying it was the letter, written in the wee hours of the morning, holding the promises from his bride to be.

Others began arriving as well, including my lifelong friend, Carol Lea, who was coming to put my makeup on. We were able to spend some time praying, and the photographer captured a special moment that, to this day, warms my heart. We sat cross-legged on the bed, facing each other, trying not to cry while recalling moments of our childhood.

A lifetime of knowing each other.

My Gift to God

A lifetime of knowing each other's heartaches, but also each other's joys, and understanding not only was I sitting here with fulfillment of promises an hour away, but she also was less than three months away from God's fulfillment in her own life, to marry her groom, Steve.

We sat, playing patty-cake, like schoolgirls, until we held each other's hands in prayer, before she helped my cousin, Leigh Anne, bring in my wedding dress to step into. They put honeysuckles in my hair and placed the veil on my head.

Lying on the bed was my Mammaw's handkerchief and the pearls that Adam had made for me nearly a decade prior. As the final adornments were placed, Caritas, my friend from Alabama, climbed the stairs to kiss me on the cheek. A few more moments passed before I quietly walked down the staircase to meet the bagpiper who would prelude my walking down the driveway, over the wooden bridge to take my daddy's arm as he escorted me into the circle of witnesses to meet my husband for our vows.

Adam and I were surrounded by those who had witnessed all of the happenings of our lives, and who had supported us throughout our lives.

It was the most serene moment, walking into that circle and looking around at everyone in attendance, standing in their commitment to uphold this long awaited union. As I took my

Adam's hand, and saw the tears in his eyes, match my own, everyone else disappeared.

I wish there were words that could encompass the rapturing of my heart that day, joining not only my husband's hand in marriage, but also acknowledging the love of Christ that was surrounding us. There is a picture capturing a moment of prayer where those witnessing our union had heads bowed and arms reaching towards us, as they all prayed. The picture depicts that moment eloquently.

It captures the pivotal moment of God's love coming full circle, as well as the restoration of our hearts.

As we spoke our vows in solidarity, we committed to love and care for each other until death do us part.

Stepping out of that circle as husband and wife, we could only smile and laugh in utter enjoyment, as we greeted our guests, and family, now, as Adam and Sarah McKinnis. The evening continued, with mouth-watering food, fellowship, toasting by our Indiana friends, Keri and Nikki, before having a bonfire and then heading down to the riverboat for our honeymoon, aboard the majestic Delta Queen.

Even the consummation of our marriage was not a lighthearted event, but rather an entering into our promises that forever was he and I and I and him.

No others would be welcome. No others would be invited.

My Gift to God

This was sacred, a union of eyes latching eyes, and hearts latching hearts, to become one as God intended in His unique design. Fun and laughter enveloped us in those moments, and continue on even now, as well, but our marriage bed became, and remains, a sacred place for two people who love, respect and adore each other.

CHAPTER 18

What is Love?

« —∞— »

IN THE PAST FIVE YEARS, MY definition of love has changed from a word I thought I understood into an action that continually unfolds before me. The concept of love is something personally, it seems I was constantly searching for, at least what my perception of what perfect love encompassed. Once the glass surrounding that word was shattered, in my younger years, the definition of love morphed to fit wherever I was, or whomever I was around, with no solid footing to stand on. Thus, as these last five years have passed, I have fully acknowledged I did not genuinely have a clear understanding of what love meant. And, the journey to the core of love has been remarkable!

Even though I know, today, both of my parents love me unconditionally, when my life went into that tailspin at age nine and continued on into my early thirties, it really felt like their love for me was conditioned on how well I behaved to their standards or accomplished certain goals. It felt conditional and something I had to strive to achieve. Having concluded my mother was sentencing me to hell for my lifestyle, it made it easy for me to not worry about trying to get her to love me, and made the ease with which I denied her, repeatedly, to be, in essence, cyclical as I felt she was pronouncing judgment against me. This allowed the hatred to fester deeply within my heart, during those two silent years, as I continued to blame her for all that had happened. I was not interested in the resolution of a loving parental relationship with her. It was quite the opposite with my father, however. His love and adoration was given freely. Until he became absent from me and present with alcohol being his first choice, once God did not heal him on his own timeframe. But, he was also the one whose attention I desired more than anything else and when I realized his attention could be especially garnered by success and achievements, I worked relentlessly to that end. Looking back, I believe this is when the word love became increasingly confusing and difficult to distinguish.

It was a word I thought I knew in those younger years, and I definitely felt love, but with that shift in all of our lives, there became no reliable context that I could grasp onto. Prior to the stroke, I was always by my daddy's side, and he would initiate conversations about my future, even at that young age. I remember him being solely focused on me realizing success in everything that I was a part of, whether that was schoolwork, learning to compete in horse shows, shooting guns, or just in general, everyday tasks. It is no wonder that I thought I could drive his truck that day in the garden, because there was so much he desired to teach me and that he wanted me to learn. It excited him to see me try new things and learn to conquer my fears, transferring the belief that looking at the world, I could accomplish anything I desired. He talked with me, openly, about dreaming for my future and unfolded his own dreams before me about building another home with a larger barn for our horses, and giving me a nice car when I turned sixteen. He would even discuss where I would go to college and who I would marry.

I remember one such conversation quite vividly, now that memories have begun to return. One day, we were out on our horses riding, and he said to me, matter of factly,

"Sarah, one day you are going to get married and love someone more than you love me."

My reply was emphatic, that I could never love anyone more than him, at which he laughed, and then he said,

"Well, when you do marry someone I hope it's someone I can talk to and maybe even have a drink with. If I'm going to have to share you, I hope I, at least, like the boy."

I replied, "Daddy, I could never marry someone you didn't like!"

He laughed again, and then we put our horses into a run in the field.

So, when you take all of that attention and affection away and you are left with a person sitting across from you that will not even put the paper down to talk to you, or turn the television off to look at you, or put the beer can down to spend any amount of time with you, or to just show up when you said you were going to be there, the word begins to not hold any clout.

To this very day, since his stroke, I have never heard the words "I love you" uttered from his mouth.

I know he loves me, because he shows me daily, with a look in his eyes or a tight hug while he calls me,

"Baby . . ." In his sweet, daddy-voice that is almost songlike when he speaks it.

But the word "love" is too difficult for his mouth to relinquish, or his tongue to form. Even though I know there is a physical aspect as to why he cannot deliver those words to my ears, my heart still aches to hear them.

One of my most precious treasures is a little 3x5 notecard tucked away in a little metal box. On it are the words "I Love You Sarah" scribbled in pencil, twice. It was given to me while my daddy was still in the hospital and while I was still convinced he was dead and everyone was lying to me. My uncle had written it out and helped my dad trace the letters, even though it didn't look very similar to his regular handwriting. He wanted to give me some kind of hope and peace. I guess, even in the midst of the tidal wave of fear, grief, and anxiety that he was experiencing, there was a realization it was traumatic to us both. My husband will tell you I speak those three little words, probably, a hundred times a day.

What is Love?

I want the people I love to always hear it and to always know it. So, love, the word, was not something very flippant to me throughout my life, even though many times my actions proved otherwise.

When my dad sobered up and the focus became my education and career, I learned when I did well, or the more success I achieved, he always wanted to share in it. I loved the attention and seeing the pride in his eyes. To this day, I acutely realize I still try my best to do things to garner that affection. I still desire to hear the words, all the while knowing he does not love me just for my successes, but just because I am his little girl.

Learning to love my mother, however, has been a greater task with much deeper roots.

Although our relationship, today, is the best it has ever been, it is so far from where we have come from, and the journey has not been easy. There are still things we do not agree on, or remember in the same light, because they are each from our own perspective. But, we do love each other, and I have learned over the years that respect and love really do go hand in hand. Sometimes, getting her to talk about key moments or details is akin to trying to open a vault without the combination, which absolutely drives me nuts. She is exceptional at asking questions, sometimes more than I want her to, but getting her to express her thoughts is altogether different.

My Gift to God

I would say this is the main reason she and I have had such difficulty, because I crave communication, especially when things are not going well. I want to understand as much as possible. Never had this been more prevalent than during that year with all of the changes with my father's health. This was the pivotal moment, where the unexplained decisions were leaving marks of my hatred and distrust towards her. My memories hold no conversations explaining what was happening when Daddy was in the hospital, no preparation for the first time I saw him and he could not hold me or talk to me, no understanding of why we had to move and, certainly, no discussion my parents would already be separated and divorcing when I came back from that trip to Florida. I was so struck by constant unexplained change, my love began turning to hate, and my respect to distrust.

The one person I always talked to could no longer talk to me, and the one I needed to talk to me, would not.

Although I had felt there was some jealousy concerning how close of a relationship I had with my daddy, prior to the stroke, I expected my mother to explain to me what was going on, after the stroke. But, this was not the case.

I wanted her to show me she loved me by just talking to me, like my daddy had always done. So, the silence just drove home how unimportant I felt to both of them. I know, looking back, she was doing all she could to keep us financially afloat and trying to protect

What is Love?

me from seeing the anger and hurt that was coming out in my dad through the excessive drinking. I do, still, vehemently believe, if she had just talked with me, it would not have turned our relationship so detrimentally. Instead, the blame replaced my concern or respect or love for her. Every single time she carted me off to have someone else talk to me, the deeper the knife went inside of me and it was always the same conversation on my part.

I wanted to know why she could not and would not talk to me.

I look back now and realize, even in my twenties, I was still trying to overcome a profound sense of aloneness. Shortly after she married Larry, Stacey and I visited Indiana, and I was trying to talk with her about what my dad was like before the stroke. My memories were severely repressed at this time, and I was attempting to persuade her to walk me through some memories in hopes I may recall some details. I wanted to know what he was like before, so that, hopefully, it would trigger some moments in my mind.

I wanted anything.

His favorite color.

What were his goals?

What did he like to eat?

Anything!

I did not care how little or minute the detail was; I just needed information.

My Gift to God

I needed memories, but she did not want to remember or to even try and help.

Even Larry, at one point, told her "I think you need to talk to your daughter about her dad." That is probably the only statement he made we had agreed on during my entire visit there. You would have thought this would not have come as a surprise to me, given our history, but all it really did was drive home the unimportance factor I felt, once again.

It is no wonder to me, today, how the devil manipulated my mind and heart about what love really was. When Stacey and I would talk, for hours and hours and hours, in the beginning, inevitably, I was so overtaken by not just the physical desires, but the emotional ones, as well. Deeply connected, the beginning of that relationship opened up all of those areas that had been lacking or I had questioned, since a little girl. When my mother called my relationship with Stacey, a situation, again, the knife was driven deeper and the distrust became a tighter woven rug to stand on. I even went to the extreme of taking my mother's engagement ring, my father had proposed to her with, and I wore it alongside a matching diamond band, Stacey and I bought, together, as a symbol of our union.

The first time my mother saw it, she attempted to rip it off my finger, and that was a pretty ugly day for both of us. I was throwing it in her face that not only was I gay, but she had purposely divorced

What is Love?

my daddy and didn't want the ring, and now it was mine. I was also using it as a symbol of my union she did not approve of, and there was nothing she could do about it.

In her face, I was in her face! And how I shake my head even right now, at how far we have come.

Like I said, the road has not been easy, for either of us.

Fast forward several years, past our silent years to when my Mammaw was in her last few weeks of life, and even then there was not much we could discuss. The damage was so irreparable that, at one point, I remember sitting in my aunt's living room with her and I had noticed every time I came in to talk to her, she would put her Bible between us. Now, granted, sometimes she was actually reading it and just closed the cover, but other times she would actually pick it up and lay it between us.

At first, I chose not to say anything and just took note of it, but then it was obvious what she was doing, so I asked her about it. I will never forget the look on her face, the words, or her expression.

I have forgiven her, but it imprinted to the core of me.

When I asked why she could not have a conversation with me without the Bible between us, she looked at me, dead in the eyes, and uttered,

"Sometimes, I just feel like I need extra protection."

I asked awkwardly, "You need protection from me?"

She looked at me, shrugged her shoulders, and nodded her head.

My Gift to God

I was speechless!! If my Mammaw had not been laying in the other room dying, I am not sure what I would have said or done that day.

The strikes against each other just kept being thrown.

Although we no longer had complete silence, we would go many months without speaking. I do not know how she felt about it, but it did not bother me because, to me, we really did not have a relationship per se, she was just who I happened to call my mother. Today, we talk every single day, but we have had a long haul of it to get here. So much baggage, and hurts not even mentioned on these pages, just piled up over the years. Even though she came to Kansas City to take care of me, during my surgery, we were still just really getting to know each other as adults. Larry had just passed away, two weeks prior, so the reprieve was timed well and I was knocked out on pain medication most of the time, so that may have helped us, as well.

Now I don't want to sound as casual as that comes across, because I was scared and I did want her there. All I am saying is we still were not where we are today. This thing they call "love," it is not always so easy, and I guess that is why, with my mother I had to learn to love her, not for simply being my mother, but as a person. I had to learn that we are two different people, and although circumstances are not always what they appear to be, if we do not understand that person's story, how can we really love them? We

What is Love?

both, in essence, had to set aside the hurts and make a decision to have a relationship, each taking responsibility for our parts in the hurts.

As you can imagine, these have not been lengthy conversations, at least on her part. However, over the last five years, the Lord has been slowly unweaving those knots in our relationship, where I do wish to talk to her daily, I do miss her when we do not speak, and I am thankful she is who God chose to be my mother.

God knew I was going to need a mother who knew how to pray and I am grateful all of those days I was silent, or hiding in the woods from her, that she never stopped loving me and prayed for God's protection over me. And, although conversations were not her forte', praying was, and is.

Hopefully, by now you can see how my perception of love became so disjointed and confusing.

I was searching for how to get it back from the time I had genuinely felt it last. When considering a child's point of view, when things flip on a dime, it is difficult, but necessary, for there to remain some sort of stability and attention. It is crucial to not just brush off their feelings because of their age or the belief that children are resilient. The impacts are much deeper than resilience, and any room for the devil to make us feel unworthy or unloved is his open door to move right into our hearts, and start imparting lies in our minds, no matter the age.

My Gift to God

Tracing back the hurts to the root of the problem is difficult, and in some situations painful, but the other side of it, when we allow God to lead us through it, is much more peaceful and beautiful than what our hearts can begin to fathom. I know this because I have experienced it first hand, over and over again, these past five years.

My loving relationship with and towards God has changed drastically and continues to evolve into something deeper as He has, with grace and mercy, unraveled my heart and mind to His truths. My parents were my two most important relationships, as that little nine-year-old girl. So, when it came to loving my Father in Heaven, I felt even His love was conditional on how "good" I behaved, or if I could even attempt to meet His standards in order to receive favor and affection. I was projecting what I had been taught or experienced onto my relationship with Him. And, even though I undeniably heard His voice speak to me, that first time as a little girl, I did not understand He was reaching out to his daughter in love, to comfort her.

I think my mother thought as long as I was going to church, I would get it somehow and I would receive all I needed there. But, in fact, I needed more. The year I spent with Clarence and Ruth, was God interjecting to introduce me to a prayer-filled home, marriage, and family life. Much like the wheels inside of a clock that keep it turning and keep it in time, they were showing through true, on your

What is Love?

knees prayer, every single morning and evening, how important that was to stay in communication with our Heavenly Father.

No prayers were too small or too big.

I can still hear Clarence praying at night in their bedroom, and although there were many times Carol Lea and I did not enjoy the prayer time every morning or being made to be up and ready every Sunday morning, the impact on both of us today remains. There is still nothing too big or too small for either of us to submit. We are not afraid to voice our prayers aloud, or to gather friends and family when we are struggling. We have both put our parents through the wringer, throughout our lives, but that time we all had, knit us together as a family. And even though I was putting on the "good" daughter face and trying my best to represent what I wanted to be, instead of what I actually felt inside, my Father in Heaven was trying to imprint His love on my heart with the provision of a safe and stable home, with two loving parents who talked to us.

Some of those conversations were not very pleasant, as I would test my boundaries with even them. At this time, Clarence was of the old school teachings that women did not wear jewelry or pants and although I was accustomed to wearing culottes at their home in the summers when I would visit, it was not the everyday norm to me. So, I began sneaking my jewelry to school. I would put it on in the school bus and take it off before he picked us up in the afternoon. One day, after he picked us up at the bus stop, we climbed into the back of their Honda, me in the middle between Carol Lea and another girl, named Sherri. I noticed Clarence kept looking at me in the rear view mirror, with this weird look on his face, and I couldn't figure it out, until Carol Lea leaned over and whispered, "You forgot to take it off."

Let me tell you about the sermon we both received when we got home that day about disrespect and lying.

I love to hear Clarence preach, but that day I did not want to hear what He was saying, as I had to hand over all of my hidden jewelry. Carol Lea and I fought like true sisters that year because just like regular siblings we tend to drag others in with us when we get in trouble. Imagine my surprise when several years ago, I see Ruth wearing jewelry and slacks and Clarence laughingly told us, "Boy, I sure did give ya'll a hard time." But both of us agree, we needed that discipline for later in our lives. We both needed a standard to hold to. We may not always agree with the discipline or sometimes, even the standards, but abiding by them, we learned to love through showing respect. It was also a lesson in realizing if someone truly cares enough to deploy instruction that bringing things out of hiding is equally as important in learning to address and deal with issues, instead of sweeping them under the rug, hoping the problem disappears.

You face the problem, address it, talk about it, and then come to a resolution. Realizing with resolution, comes compromise on each

What is Love?

person's part, although it may be uncomfortable, in the end, it produces respect when the resolution is upheld.

I can see now how paramount that year was in developing, and feeding, that need of mine for communication in a healthy manner, to face difficult situations and not just completely shut down, like I had been doing to compensate for my hurt. I was also introduced that year to the Holy Spirit, and the effect the spirit had on that little country church and its members. I had befriended a girl named Robin and spent a lot of time with her, and her family, going to their house after church, or after school, and I became pretty close to them. One Sunday evening, we were going to experience an old-fashioned, humble, action of Christ when we partnered up to wash each other's feet, like Jesus had washed the disciple's feet.

Clarence preached and then Judy, Robin's mom, grabbed my hand, asking if she could wash my feet. Right now, I can close my eyes and picture her face, her hands and hear her prayers while doing this simple, but intimate, act of friendship and love. I washed her feet also, but do not remember much of that, because while she had been washing mine, I experienced what would become my first affiliation of the Holy Spirit coming into me.

I did not fall out into the aisle, that day, rather, it was quiet, in my spirit, no yelling, no proclamation, just a soft speaking in tongues I did not know. Over the course of that year, the development of my relationship with the Holy Spirit was one I desperately desired and wanted more of, to know the peaceful coexistence that would overtake me.

The only problem with this was I kept wondering if I was committing blasphemy, because I could feel the spirit at church, but at night, when I was alone in my bedroom, the memories of my childhood orientation into sexual intimacy was overtaking my mind. That is when I really began to think I was the devil.

It was confusing how I could feel so peaceful one minute, and then the next, be staring in the mirror wondering who I was that I could have committed such acts, or been involved with my cousin, especially a female. So, it was easy to put on the mask every day to be "good" in hopes God would give me more of the Holy Spirit to wipe out the conversations in my head telling me, "If only everyone knew," and I began to learn how to hide my true emotions.

But, God was leaving His footprint so as time went on, I would know the Holy Spirit and the voice. He wanted me to experience the overtaking peace that comes from that unexplainable place.

God was pursuing me at the pace, and with those finite moments, that are only His. He knew what I needed, and precisely when I needed it. He was fighting for me, when I did not even know it, just like Exodus 14:14 says: "The Lord will fight for you, you need only be still." He was fighting for me, when I did not even know there was a fight to be had, and He was stilling me, even though I did not recognize that, either. He took me to this place, with this family, to

What is Love?

mark me as His own so later, when the fight became much more intense, He would have memories in my heart to combat what the devil was dishing out to me.

After returning home, from that year, while I no longer had the disciplined, prayerful home life, I could still pull from the impact I had been exposed to. Although my relationship with the Holy Spirit became increasingly less intentional, the impartation of that voice was something I recognized when I heard it. In those early teenage years, I became sexually active with my boyfriend, trying my best to suppress my desires for girls. I was determined to try and silence the conversations that told me I was not good enough, or that I was unlovable, if anyone were to know the truth . . .

So, I began to attempt to replace that voice and dumb it down as much as possible, by trying to be "good" or "perfect" to everyone outside of my house. There was only one obstacle, and that was when I was at home.

Thankfully, when I returned, there was a lady named Brenda, who lived with my mom and me. She had been living with us for several years, after her husband had been tragically killed in a car accident, and she had a pretty intrinsic and unique influence on my life. Because she had known me for many years, and was there on a daily basis, there was an established, trusting relationship between the two of us. She would be the first to call me out on the things I was doing, and ironically enough, I trusted her more than I did my mother, so sometimes her voice would break through to speak truth on my life. Her background was much different than my mother's, and life had taken her down many different roads, so she could associate and recognize, providing influence on me when it was needed most.

She tried to lessen the blow and be the mediator, many times when things got bad between my mother and me. But, she also held a firm stance when I was putting on the double "face." This had to be a challenge for her, but I appreciate the love she showed me, even in my obstinacy. When I turned eighteen and left the house, she probably felt some sort of relief that my mother and I were no longer under the same roof. Here, again, it was another interjection into my life of someone showing me love, while at the same time, not taking my crap.

In fact, she was the first person to know about my relationship with Stacey, and she wrote me a letter that said she did not understand it, but she loved me and wanted my happiness, above all else, because she had seen how much I had struggled with love over the years.

My leaving that house ushered in a new era of independence for me, and the word "love" would change, once again. Because along with becoming a "legal" adult, which I say very loosely, I had no idea what I was doing other than escaping my present hell with my mother. I wanted out, and thankfully, God placed me in the home with Stan and Cathy. Once again, God placed influencers to teach me what a God-centered, fun-filled marriage looked like with those whom I could talk very openly about anything I felt comfortable with.

They knew the struggles with my mom were real, and they knew the longing I had for my father's attention. They both tried their very best to be there for me through all things, including all of my relationships. Here, again, they did not always understand my choices, but chose to love me, first and foremost.

All of these people God placed into my life was unique. He placed each of them, at that time, to ensure I was exposed to some outlet of love, or to fill gaps that needed filling.

When my dad was arrested and sent to the Tennessee Veterans Home for rehabilitation, it was Cathy who suggested I attend MTSU to be near him. Sometimes, I jokingly say that is when I became a parent, but, really, this is when daddy and I began to learn to try and take care of each other. All the while, we were both so stubborn and independent that we collided tragically over the years. I finally had my daddy back, and his full attention, and I loved that, even though I did not really know what to do with it.

This was a tricky time in my life, as I was left to my own devices, learning to make decisions, some I wish I had chosen differently, but I began trying to make logical, rational choices. The next morphing of the word love involved my eight-year relationship with Dawson. We were more business partners than life partners. Even our decision to get married was just that. It was a decision and more a financial one than a relational one.

I loved him and knew, unequivocally, that he loved me deeply; but there was no part of me that was "in-love" with him. I wanted to get married simply so we were not tagged as "those people, living in sin" and have to feel the judgment of my family. Dawson was, and is, a good man. He just was not the husband who God intended for me and, in fact, God was not anywhere in the midst of that relationship.

Although we had become intimate early in our relationship, even that was pretty sketchy. At first, it was fine, but the more condemnation I felt about not being married, the less I wanted that aspect of our life. Cathy was the only person aware of my deep-seated struggles regarding those intimate details, and she knew eventually I would end up giving in, just because. My desires for women were still so prominent, and because of certain influences of people in our lives at the time, the rearing of this began strengthening inside of me, especially the last two years we were together. Intimacy, did not mean love, but rather, purely a reflection of something I had to do. When we made the decision to get married, I had resolved myself to the fact this was just how relationships were, and we had been together for so long we would figure it all out as we went.

What is Love?

How far my relationship had gone from my Heavenly Father.

I wish I had trusted that I could have endured the backlash from people and walked out of the church that day prior to our vows being spoken, versus breaking the covenant I chose to take on our wedding day.

Can you see how the definition of love was influenced and repeatedly changed into something that was depreciating in value? Because I see it more clearly, now, than ever before, when reflecting back.

It is no wonder, when Stacey came to me that evening, it was easy in a week's time to leave the marriage, the farm, and those eight years like dust in the wind. It became an ignition and an awakening that fulfilled desires and longings of communication, for not only my body but for some extremely deep sustenance, that someone could actually hear me and understand me.

It was, the hastiest life decision I have ever made.

No longer was it Dawson, my dad, and I. Now, it was Stacey, my dad, and I. And since Daddy was now living in an apartment, instead of under the same roof with me, no one had to know, at least for a little while. I hurt several people and lost friendships during that time, but chose not to consider those consequences, because I felt so alive inside.

At least for a little while, I felt alive.

My Gift to God

People sometimes ask, "Did you really love her?" And I did, absolutely, unequivocally, love her.

She was, in fact, the very first person I ever fully loved.

This is going to be difficult for some Christians to read, but this is the story of how God reached my mind, captured my heart, and showed me what unquestionable love was. Without the capability to be vulnerable, raw, and truthful about the authenticity of these feelings, then I see no purpose in this book.

So, yes, I did love her, intimately and deeply.

Even though the relationship became abusive, there were some positives that manifested in it as well. For eight years, I had not prayed or been to church, and together, she and I would pray. We attended church even though we were hiding our relationship in the beginning, and we committed our relationship to God. We desired, together, God's presence and wanted that part of our life we had both been missing since our younger years. Having experienced such similar encounters with the Holy Spirit, we desired to be close in relationship and rapport with both Jesus and God. The sincerity with which we dedicated our lives and relationship was heartfelt, and we honestly trusted the prayer we prayed about God taking our feelings towards each other away, if it was not of Him.

When He did not take it from either one of us, well, then I was all in for the long haul with her. We committed to a life together.

What is Love?

When the abuse started, I just shrugged it off at first. Or, at least, I tried to, because our good times were so good they overpowered the bad. And, as quickly as the rage inside her that produced the abuse would come to life, it would vanish just as instantly. She would apologize and dote on me to try and make things better, which I see now as compensation instead of remorse.

Our love, especially the first couple of years, seemed pretty powerful. At some point, people in the church began catching on. Truthfully, we were getting more comfortable being out and about with our relationship, so we were not hiding as much. The stares and whispered conversations drove us out of the church walls. The one place I kept hearing, from the pulpit, as the only place I would receive authentic love, was the one opening the exit doors for me to go right back out into the world, telling me not to come back in until I had pulled myself together. I wanted to be there, but as long as she was with me, we were only welcomed so far in.

The judgment was overwhelming, and left the alarming impression that, in order to receive this authentic love they were talking about, and that I remembered distantly, it was not attainable unless I came into the church as they expected me to be.

Cleaned up and without blemish.

But, heck, I did not think I was that dirty. I mean, I was not calling myself the devil in the mirror anymore, so I thought that was a good step in the right direction.

My Gift to God

Eventually, it became too uncomfortable to grace the doors of the church, so we began creating our own life away from those many restrictions. We courted places that had no problem accepting us just as we were. I will never forget the first gay bar we ever went into. I had only been in one or two bars by this time in my life and did not have much experience drinking alcohol on a regular basis, nor did I have the desire to. To put it as plainly as possible, it was weird and uncomfortable to me. I did not really want to be there, at first, except it was the one place she could hold my hand or kiss me without funny looks from everyone. And everybody was there for the same reason; we did not have to hide and we would not get kicked out or end up in a fight about our lifestyle.

But, one bar turned into another and then another until, eventually, it was our normal routine on the weekends, and so was the drinking. It became easy, and when the abuse progressed, the alcohol just helped me to forget.

My places of safety were beginning to dwindle, and again, love transitioned from something I just had, or felt naturally, to something I had to perform well at or meet certain standards in order to receive. This was tantamount in my relationship with her, in the church, and subsequently, with some of my family. The only exceptions were a select handful of people. But, not even one of those people knew about the abuse and the toll it was taking on me as the years passed and the intensity of it evolved.

What is Love?

The standards I ultimately would have to attain to avoid a beating became too complex and lofty to possibly achieve. With the end of that relationship was still this desire to just be known and to be loved fully, but the segregation from everyone had left me holding little trust or confidence in anyone personally. When I began figuring out who I really was and what I liked, it was exhilarating and stimulating.

Subsequently, during the next eight years of my life, love morphed into whatever made me happy in the moment. The boldness with which I refused to care how my actions affected others was all for my protection's sake, as I was adamant to not open myself up for someone to know the vulnerable side of my heart. With the exception of the devil kicking me in the gut with Brian's analysis of me being unsafe around his teenage daughter, I did pretty well at keeping everyone just close enough, but not too close. Love became something I could control and give out only as I saw fit.

Who knew I would dish out what I felt love really was, with conditions and on specific standards being met, while I held the rest of it in reserve, under lock and key? I was becoming the very thing I despised, hard hearted and cold.

God knew I had no idea what authentic love was, and He also knew how close to the end of the rope I was that August, when He set His plan in motion to open my eyes, and then to open my mind, before I would be able to open my heart, to Him or anyone else.

My Gift to God

That is the only way He could meet me, and it was His plan all along.

His pursuit of me came through interjections throughout my life that were so intrinsically placed to reach me at various times so I would still know who He was. No matter how far I tried to run or how deep I tried to dive in escape, His quest was for me to know not only did a real God exist, but that He desired my heart with no strings attached. All of these various experiences throughout my life had drastically shifted what I thought authentic love was. With my history and the way I am wired, He knew communication was going to be the key to undeniable revelation of the truth, and to clear up any confusion that continued to reside inside of me.

He accomplished this by using that same verse from Exodus 14:14, I mentioned earlier.

He needed me to be still, literally, to show me I was worth fighting for.

He was coming for His daughter, to reveal to her the truth throughout scripture, with zero interruptions.

He not only began to debunk the lies I had believed, and the banners I had erected and called truths, but also He began weaving a tapestry of love and truth that He lovingly draped around me.

He did not beat me over the head with the Bible, He just asked me to open it.

What is Love?

He did not yell at me and shake his fist, telling me I was not gay, He showed me why I thought I was.

He showed me the root to why I felt certain things throughout my life, and that there was a valid reason I felt I was gay. My attraction was very real, and well, it should have been, because it was my first introduction into how to show someone I loved them, or so I was taught as a six-year-old.

I had no idea, until just a few years ago, as the memories continued to unfold, that it was not just me and my cousin in those rooms. There were two others there, who were making us play games with each other, so we could express how much we liked and loved each other.

So, standing on the fact I had felt like I was gay since a little girl, was rooted in truth.

God was the only one who could reveal these moments that had impacted me so greatly, and then show me the real truth of it all.

I just had to be a willing participant, to listen and to follow His lead and not try to open doors I was not ready for.

I had to be willing to sit still, and to listen to Him, and become comfortable in being alone in His presence.

That was where He met me, exactly where I was, with the truth of my life before me. He did not want me to clean up my act, or get it all together, in order that I may receive His love and blessings.

My Gift to God

He wanted me to sit before Him, just as I was, and bestow love and mercy on me, in His truth, to feel the real deal.

He has, and is, and continues to reveal depths to that word, love that I am still learning. But, I learn by listening and by Him loving me first, before I can even attempt to model what it is He has shown me. And, God has revealed Himself to be the epitome of what Paul describes as love in 1 Corinthians 13:

"And now I will show you the most excellent way. If I speak in the tongues of men and of angels, but have not love, I am only a resounding gong or a clanging cymbal. If I have the gift of prophecy and can fathom all mysteries and all knowledge, and if I have a faith that can move mountains, but have not love, I am nothing. If I give all I possess to the poor and surrender my body to the flames, but have not love, I gain nothing. Love is patient, love is kind, it does not envy, it does not boast, it is not proud. It is not rude, it is not self-seeking, it is not easily angered, it keeps no record of wrongs. Love does not delight in evil but rejoices with the truth. It always protects, always trusts, always hopes, always perseveres. Love never fails. But where there are prophecies they will cease; where there are tongues, they will be stilled; where there is knowledge, it will pass away. For we know in part and we prophecy in part, but when perfection comes, the imperfect disappears. When I was a child, I thought like a child, I reasoned like a child. When I became a man, I put childish ways behind me. Now we see but a poor reflection as in a mirror; then we shall see face to face. Now I know in part; then I shall know fully, even as I am fully known. And now these three remain: faith, hope and love. But the greatest of these is love."

When I realized Jesus came in order that we may know true love from God, and there was no way I could ever even attempt to be perfect enough in order to receive His love, and it just did not work that way, I was released!

I was released, to not try to gain His love and attention, but to just be able to sit and receive it.

I was released, to be able to hear Him ask me if I trusted Him enough to give everything to Him.

He was loving me, just as I was, and just as I am.

This is the love I came to know before marrying Adam, and that I attempt to show him daily. It is the type of love my Abba Father has shown me, and He continues to do so. Adam and I have a love based on respect and truth and, most of all, love. Our marriage is so much better than I ever anticipated, because we mutually ascribe to this. And no, our marriage is not perfect and there have been some things we just did not want to bring to light at first, but the more we do bring to light and the longer we have been married and keep trusting in that love, trust, and respect formula, the better it gets. This has even impacted the intimacy aspect of our marriage. It is not utilized as a game or something that has to be done, it is something we mutually desire and we both realize what a gift it is to be fun-loving and respectful in giving each other, fully, our inner most desires as a couple.

Never once has he perversely turned my past into a joke, and I crave his affection as much as he craves mine.

God really did make us for each other, and I am so thankful to know that my Abba Father is in all the details of love!

CHAPTER 19

Becoming a Daughter
« —∞— »

THIS MORNING, AS I WRITE THIS chapter, I am sitting in the mountains of North Carolina. There is an early morning fog that has been rolling over the lake that has captivated my attention. It slowly meanders through the curves of the water, and then begins to twist and turn, like a dancer, before climbing up through the trees into the mountaintops, slowly disappearing, revealing a crisp, baby blue sky. The fog is lifting ever so slowly, and I realize, once again, how much God is really interested in all of the details of each of His children. Being on the water, whether it be stream, lake, river, or ocean, they each calm me and slow me down to reflect on His magnificence. Sitting in stillness, for hours, is quite easy for me during these moments, and I sometimes just simply say,

"Thank You Lord, for everything you have done throughout my life, even when I did not acknowledge you."

His evidence is everywhere to me, and although I realize there are certain circumstances that could have played out differently in my life, He was the constant source of fluidity that kept me going.

My Gift to God

As I would skip along the top of the water and jump from tree to tree with little concern, occasionally my feet would land in the cool, crisp waters of His love, where He would carry me for a while and then release me again, to my own devices and to find my own way. Each interaction left its mark on me, and I knew I could always come back for more sustenance. He then began enticing me to not just dip my feet, but to submerge in the waters and feel the depth of His love, so He could begin to wash my heart with His words and His truth. He desired to encompass me fully, show me that I could trust Him, and never would there come a time I would be taken deeper than I was ready for, or to visit places He had not already prepared for me.

The deeper I allowed Him to lovingly take me, the more I realized how long I had believed I could only be loved so much. He wanted to show me a parental love, so pure and unconditional, that never would He leave me, or had ever left me. In those moments, where I had felt most alone, He even showed me where He was in those times, and I was neither forgotten nor forsaken, as I had believed.

He showed me that He is my Father and that I am his daughter.

My willingness to give Him everything, and to trust Him with all of it, was a slow process, but, always faithful to His promises, He continues to keep me safe. Each time I break back through the water and come up for air, I see the world with new eyes. Just as the fog lifts into the sky and reveals that crisp, blue sky, He will release me once again, to go dance among the trees carrying His love with me.

It has been an amazing journey and one I look forward to every single day, now, because I know His work in me is so far from complete. I am still learning it does not matter to Him how big or small the mountains of questions I have asked over these last several years, because He will speak to me when I choose to listen. Never has this been more apparent than several months after Adam and I got married. I was attending a ministry leadership conference back in Kansas City, ironically enough.

It was my first visit back, but the only person I would see that I knew was Pastor James. He picked me up at the airport and drove me out to this beautiful retreat site, with cabins and trails, where the conference was held. Truthfully, I had absolutely no idea what I was in for, that week, other than this was something both Pastor James, and Pastor John from Harmony Vineyard, felt God wanted for me to attend. My assessment from the research and application process, which they both helped me with, was that I was going to learn to minister to those who had experienced relational brokenness.

Trust me, I thought it sounded as weird, at the time, as it may appear to you as you read this.

I had no concept of what relational brokenness meant, nor how it truly related to me. I knew there would be connections to my experiences as a child, and an adult, sexually, and how they impacted each other. Kind of a connect the dots to form the picture type deal. My assumptions of how my days would unfold, and the depth of love I would experience, were at opposite ends of the spectrum. I thought I was there to learn a curriculum, and was prepared for that, and to be able to come back and do whatever it was God wanted me to do, but that was not what He had prepared for me that week.

I was there to be taught, but not the curriculum. He was about to teach me how to become His child.

James and I sat underneath a pavilion looking out over a meadow lined with trees, when we arrived at the retreat location. I remember listening to the rustle of the wind, and watching the colorful leaves begin to drift away from their branches, until coming to rest on the ground below. It was really beautiful that day, and the entire week, as I came to be acquainted with several of the other participants over the course of our time together, all coming from varied places in the country and across the world.

But, here, I sat with this man, who God had placed in my life not long after moving to Kansas City.

A man who, just like Stan and Clarence from my youth, had been placed as a fatherly influence in my life.

A man who had felt, inexplicably, that God had told him to love me like a father, so much so, that he and his wife Wanda had asked me into their family.

Becoming a Daughter

A man who, although our skin is a different color, loves me as if I were of his own flesh and blood.

A man who was sitting here beside this girl, who really did not know how to receive the love of a father, and he was speaking to me softly, and delivering prayers and gentle words of wisdom.

He told me he knew I was expectant of what I was about to enter into that week. He also understood doing a good job, or doing things well, was usually my approach, but he wanted me to approach this week a little differently.

With his tender wisdom, James asked that I not be expectant, but rather that I be willing.

In agreement with him to do just that, I could not have envisioned what this week was going to hold for me. After he left me there, to check in and get settled into my cabin, I took a long walk through the woods and came upon a meadow, with these three beautiful, rustic, rugged crosses. All I desired at that moment was to sit in silence.

It was quiet and peaceful sitting there, praying a prayer of willingness and thankfulness, until it was time to gather myself back together and walk, slowly, down the little narrow path through the trees back towards the cabin. Each day I would visit those crosses, and each day a little more would be revealed to my heart, as I learned to lay things down at the foot of the cross.

My Gift to God

Getting my bearings, that first evening, on how things were to operate for the week, taking in the surroundings and introducing myself to my cabin mates was a bit awkward, at first. But, eventually, it was time to walk up the hill to the dining cabin to eat a meal with strangers, before finally meeting the leaders of the conference and learning the logistics of the conference. We were each given large manuals of information we would take home with us. Wanting to be prepared for the next day's teaching, I went back to my room, laid on the bed, and commenced reading and studying diligently.

I had not quite come to understand the willing part, just yet.

The next morning I awoke early, to shower and take another stroll in solitude, before, once again, visiting the dining cabin. I found myself at the table with the same five people from the evening before. We were getting comfortable with each other over eggs, bacon, coffee and a multitude of other food choices and then, it was time for our first real meeting or teaching. Returning to my cabin after partaking in breakfast, I grabbed the manual and a notebook, ready to embark on this journey. I climbed the hill, entered the meeting room, and migrated to sit next to my eating mates, waiting expectantly.

When the teaching started, I was a little confused as to how we were being taught. I mean, were we not going to go through this big book I had carried over here, and that lay open in my lap?

Becoming a Daughter

In a small state of confusion, I listened as the instructor, for this session, began sharing about their life and, although the information in the manual was covered, I quickly gathered this week was not going to be about power point presentations. The manual covered a twelve-week program, and I was about to experience those twelve weeks in seven days. This week was considered a leadership retreat in which we would be released afterwards to minister to others, but instead of just receiving instruction on how to minister, we were going to be ministered to. It proved to be like an inner healing program on steroids.

And, God, knew I needed it that way.

He knew my heart needed to be enveloped in a ministry time so concentrated I could not run, in order to feel His overwhelming love for me.

Twice a day, we met for worship, prayer, teaching, and then our small groups would meet. After dinner, each day ended with a ministry time that is incomprehensible in the words of these small sentences.

After that first teaching was over, it was very quiet in the room. Although we had some ministry time, we were then introduced to our small groups, as well as our small group leader. I did not realize how prayerfully planned these groups were, until much later in the week. My group all came together and we awkwardly walked to our meeting location, in a secluded loft. We sat in a circle and our sweet, loving, group leader, Ann, led us in prayer, then explained the group dynamics, prior to us each taking turns introducing ourselves.

And then, the willingness that James had spoken to me about became front and center.

Ann, in her gentle, humble demeanor, talked with us about sharing why we were there, and how the earlier teaching impacted us. We began to become intimately aware of each other's journeys through life and every single person's journey was unique. Not all had experienced sexual abuse or was a homosexual like me, but there was a sacred resonating sense of safety for each and every single person there. Our personal exposure was only at our most vital comfort level and there was such a replenishment to our soul of things the devil had tried to take from each person over the years. That week was just that, for me. Twice a day, we met and shared with each other. For the first time, I was allowed to sit safely and just talk, spilling secrets only Adam had ever been privy to.

Hurts from my childhood came gushing out, unexpectedly, like winter pipes that had burst open. For the first time in my life, I was released from the pain and the brokenness I had tried so hard, as a six, seven, eight, and nine-year-old little girl, to just keep to myself, pretending everything was fine or pretending it had never even happened.

The lie, that I could trust no one and depend on solely myself for protection, was no longer encapsulating my heart.

Becoming a Daughter

My personal experience was not one I anticipated being so open about, especially with complete strangers. But by the end of the week not only did I experienced a group of women fighting in prayer for me in my small group, as well as the five men and women, from all over the country, becoming close friends, while sharing meals and sitting together in sessions. None of us previously knew each other, and although we were not in each other's small groups, we became like a family that week. To this day we remain in contact with each other. We revel in watching God's promises fulfilled, of marriages and babies being born, ministry opportunities in the states, as well as in Africa, among so many other things.

Even more than all of that, was the simplicity of being completely alone with God.

Although Adam and I were married and I knew that was not the end to the story, I still understood I was craving more.

Adam fulfills my personal, physical, and soul cravings for an earthly relationship, but there was, still, this abyss of hurt that needed filling that may only be accomplished by allowing an opening up, and a drilling out, of that which has been tarnished throughout life. Then, God can sift out the lies and the deception to reach the core of the truth, and begin rebuilding that which has been torn away.

I could not have anticipated when God's inner healing began to enrapture my heart, I would long to become a child, if only I would allow it and be willing.

My Gift to God

Below is one of my journal entries I wrote while there that week:

As a child, I did not want to make my daddy feel bad for not being around. I guess I expected my mom to pick up the parts and keep our lives somewhat normal. I expected her to be there for me, and she was not, I wanted him there, and he was not. I started taking care of myself and not allowing anyone else to do that for me. I carried that forward until my surgery last year. It is still very hard for me to get upset with my dad because each time I start to feel guilty, because he was the one who suffered the stroke. It is much easier to get upset with my mom, although over this past year, God has begun to show me her vulnerability and also started making me a much more compassionate person for her, with her and in general thoughts of her. I felt guilty because, even into my twenties, I always thought if my dad had not had his stroke, my life would be so different. I felt like I had lost him in so many ways, to the stroke and then again, to alcohol, until finally, one day I realized he is right there in front of me. I have still felt guilty for grieving my loss of what we were before the stroke, and the dreams he used to share with me, and how different things were afterward. I felt left with my mother, who had become bitter and unavailable, with no concern for keeping things the way they used to be, when in reality she was doing all she knew to do. But I DO miss my mom and I DO miss my dad . . . I grieve it and today, I give it to you, God, because they are both present in my life. They are not gone. They are both alive and I ask forgiveness for those grievances.

God, in His mercy, took me back to this very real place of hurt and distrust to reveal to my heart I still longed to be that little girl and I had been grieving my lost childhood. He also showed me every other relationship I have had suffered because of that distrust. In one of the ministry times, while I was praying, He showed me a picture. I was sitting on the floor, with my head in my mother's lap, and she was brushing my hair with her hands.

Such a simple, but intimate, act of love and I realized I could not remember the last time I would have even allowed her to get that close to me.

Sure, I would let her give me a hug, but even those better not be too tight, or for too long.

I knew these boundaries had been erected for people, regarding how close they could get to me, and He was attempting to show me that we could either take them down brick by brick, or I could choose to dive in and let him take them all the way down. And, with an intentional, resolute prayer of willingness, I decided, I wanted it all!

How could I allow the fact that Jesus had come to this earth, endured the slashing of stripes, and crucifixion on the cross so that I my heart may be healed, but then not be willing for these deep hurts to be mended?!!

My Gift to God

As I visited those three crosses each day, alone, Jesus would meet me there. I would begin to lay each issue down, as He revealed what I was struggling with, and as I would give it to Him, the more freedom overtook my heart, of things I no longer had to hold onto.

Prior to leaving that week, the five of us who had been sharing our meals together, walked to that field with the crosses for the first time, together. We sat and prayed prayers of blessings over each other, and it was just a very sweet, innocent time. It was like we were all learning to be children. Although I do not know the individual impacts that week had on each of them, I know there was a peace resting over that entire retreat.

Coming back home was difficult because I had to re-acclimate to normal, everyday life, and the noise was deafening.

I had been immersed in this week of no external noises, except people talking quietly and our worship music at night. When I arrived at the airport, phones were ringing, the television was blaring and the intercom system never seemed to be empty of announcements. All of it kept sounding off in my head before being rounded up into a metal airplane with engines and crying babies, I, literally, felt dizzy from the over-stimulation.

Adam probably thought, "Where did my wife go?", because I was so overwhelmed that I did not have a lot to say, when he took me to dinner after picking me up from the airport. There was so much that had blown my socks off and I wanted to share with him, but the sensitivity of my senses was on complete overload. Even after we got home, I did not turn the television on for a couple of weeks.

I know it sounds bizarre and crazy, but it made me conscious of how desensitized we are in life. All of the sounds coming at us from every direction and it is no wonder we have so many people walking around that cannot hear God's voice.

The confusion is too much and I am glad that neither Adam nor I have a problem with enjoying the quiet and having alone time.

But also, upon my return, I was craving that solitary time of prayer and meditation with my Father. Once again He ignited in me a desire and He was beckoning me to continue to come closer, so we may come to know each other. He was not trying to "fix" me. Just as marrying Adam did not "fix" me from being a homosexual, neither did The Living Waters retreat become a "fixing" process either. He was drawing me close in communion with Him.

He had provided this safe environment at the retreat, so I could be introduced to true and authentic love, grace, and mercy from God. The retreat was not just to teach us how to minister, but to learn how to come into this communion with God that is so relationally humble, and stripped down to the bare bones of just Him and just me. I had never experienced the depths of relationship, in that manner and that, ultimately, has ushered in the depths of healing and communication I feel with my Father in Heaven to this day.

My Gift to God

The depth of mercy I experienced and the openness to mourn a childhood I did not acknowledge, that I felt like I had lost, was really just the beginning.

He had even already prepared a place for me to meet him on a weekly basis.

There was a new place in downtown Chattanooga that our pastor, Dale, introduced me to; ChattHOP, or Chattanooga House of Prayer. For over a year, I would spend my Tuesday mornings and afternoons there, tucked away on the third floor of this renovated warehouse space, with a beautiful soul named MickiAnn, who was in charge of the prayer room.

The cool thing about that time and space was not only having time alone, focused on prayer and worship, but I also got to know MickiAnn and the humility she exudes. We did not have very many lengthy discussions, but each time we talked, the conversations were intentional. We were always digging deeper into the Father's Heart. The peace in that place was palpable, and sometimes, I would steal away up a metal staircase to a little rooftop garden. There, I would just stand in awe because no longer was He having to pursue me, I was now pursuing Him.

I wanted more.

He had proven to me that, although there were some pretty difficult places that needed revisiting from my life, if I allowed Him to, Jesus would walk me back to each of those places. He would open my heart and soul to whatever needed to be set right. And, even when some of those were very emotional and deep hurts, I would not be left there alone for it to overtake me, because the grace and protection of Jesus Christ was always there. I would be shown where God was, during that time, before walking me right back out of it and filling that emptiness with His love and truth. My part in it all was simply to be willing and to know I was His daughter, and never would He hurt me.

He was changing my heart and is still, today, changing my heart.

Six months after attending the Living Waters retreat, they called to ask if I would pray about coming to serve on their leadership team for the upcoming retreat. After some prayer and talking with Adam about it, I agreed. I was ecstatic to be able to enter another week of that communion, even though in a different role this time, as a co-leader of one of the small groups. I was expectant and anticipated being able to witness the love of my Father being shown to others. And to watch the postural changes of hearts releasing heaviness to the one true comforter, while being able to stand with my own shoulders back before Him. I was also anxious for the immersion of His presence to overwhelm us all, and had been setting aside time to pray for the other team members, as well as the participants.

Again, I had no idea what to expect. And, once again, He was about to show me He desired to take me deeper still.

My Gift to God

All of the leadership team stayed together. We were paired with roommates, with a common area where we would meet prior to every teaching for an intentional time of prayer, together, as a group. Three times a day, we met in this big circle and, as a newbie, I was completely unprepared for what was coming my way.

If I was desiring communion with God, I was about to witness how caring He is, but also how intentional prayer could get straight to the heart of things, quickly.

Dean or Ann, who were the leaders of the leadership team, always opened us up in prayer and they would lead us into a three-part prayer, where anyone from the team could speak out in prayer, if they felt led to do so. There was absolutely no obligation we had to participate. We would thank God for whatever was on our hearts, ask forgiveness for whatever we felt we needed to, personally, and then lift up our prayer requests and pray for each other, as well.

This was authentic, verbal, open communion and something I knew absolutely nothing about. I learned that God needed us to do this, in order that we could enter into each session with clean hearts and clean minds, solely focused on what it was God wanted to do. This time eliminated the distractions that could potentially interfere with being able to minister to the participants, or that would block us from hearing God's voice. I was witnessing a group of people that desired the heart of the Father so much they were willing to be wholly vulnerable with no secrets.

Asking forgiveness had always been something I just did alone or silently, and this group was an open book, with intimate only God knowing things that they were verbalizing forgiveness for.

It took me a long minute to gather myself together!

Never was there a conversation or remark as to why someone asked forgiveness for a certain thing, it was just a safe place to be vulnerable. But, what I was learning was they were not doing it for themselves, they were doing it so God's love could flow through them with ease, and so His children could encounter this authentic love, grace and mercy!

They were being servants and nothing more, and now everything I had experienced as a participant made sense to me, because there had been this team of people who were laying down their everything in order that I, and the others, were able to receive. God was now inviting me into this circle to, again, take me deeper still, not just in my relationship with Him but to intimately learn what it meant to be a servant to others.

Over the course of the week, I became exceedingly more comfortable with this prayer model. I allowed the vulnerability to present itself, because it was not for me. My heart was turning to the hearts of my brothers and sisters, that they may experience everything God had so graciously done for me and more.

This was, unquestionably, the deepest I had ever experienced a relationship and witnessing the vulnerability and honesty did not produce judgment, but rather blessings, manifesting right before my eyes, intrigued me to go and seek the depths of my Father's heart without fear.

I served with the leadership team one more time, as a group leader, a year later and, again, it was a dive into the waters to go as deep as possible. One of the many things I am so honored God would show me was it was not about developing programs, but more about being a facilitator that gets to the core of who we each are, individually, and releasing those pent-up hurts to be healed so we could walk out the life and callings God created us for.

And, only God can do that, we cannot do it on our own, and the deepness He wants us to trust Him with is so we will not to be able to forget the encounter of true love.

It was not my homosexuality that needed healing; it was the hurts in my heart that I did not even know were there.

And God, in only His loving way, has, over the past five years, taken me back to some pretty difficult places. When He asked me if I trusted Him enough to give everything to Him, I had no idea what was being orchestrated.

Even though I was genuinely willing to give everything over to Him, it was a process, especially for someone who had become accustomed to their way or the highway. It would prove to be a lesson in humility, pure love, and restoration.

Becoming a Daughter

Getting married was definitely not the end of this story, but rather a long acknowledgment of God's fulfillment of promises. Because getting married is not what "fixes" those who are homosexual. And, "fixing" is such a negative connotation anyway. Just as I despised my mother for telling me that she was glad I was better, inclined my mind to wonder "What did she think I was better from?" I do still believe all that I have gone through has made me who I am today. My love for God is not because He fixed me, but rather because He loved me no matter the choices that I made in life, and that He continues to pursue me although my memories and my heart were blinded from what truth really was and what it is.

What changed, in my life, was that I was willing to surrender, and to put all other thoughts and feelings in the arms of my Maker, so that He could reveal to me the rights and wrongs. Just as the scripture in Ezekiel says, "He will give me a new heart and a new spirit." There was not one single, little or big, thing I could do to make that happen; it was and still is a long and arduous process.

But, when God is leading the change, the love, grace, and mercy so overpower the hurt it does not become something you have to endure, but rather something to look forward to.

CHAPTER 20

Learning Forgiveness
« —∞— »

SERVING ON THE LEADERSHIP team, both times, had softened my heart to servitude and seeking for others, instead of seeking for myself, but I was quite surprised at the impact of what I would receive, as well. There had been no expectations to receive anything, actually, but being submerged in these week long, intensely deep, ministry times, I am unsure of why I was surprised. Maybe, because I was more focused outward to others, versus inward, He decided it was time to rip another Band-Aid off and apply some more ointment.

I have come to realize I can never figure His plan out and have decided I do not want to, because if I knew ahead of time, it would probably make me run the other direction. What He would present in front of me to face, was definitely not on the radar of anything I thought I had a problem with, or that I felt deserved focused consideration.

But, God.

He wanted to reorient my conception of forgiveness and replace it with a trajectory deeper than a superficial, surface level of forgiveness.

He desired a change on my heart that would culminate from the willingness to participate in confronting those hidden, deep-rooted caverns that held no light. Demolishing walls, once again, to let pure light in, He could expose truth and love while extinguishing the hurts, my heart had endured. He desired the change that would be a result of the willingness to trust Him so He could prepare the way for His plans. And, how could I really extend grace and mercy to anyone else if I did not have forgiveness to offer when warranted?

The challenge was who He wanted me to forgive, because it was not who I expected.

I knew, over the course of my life, I had built some pretty stout walls with the largest bricks I could find, in order to protect myself. However, He was telling me that, although He was glad I had tried to take care of myself and had shown me some grace in that, they were no longer needed. He was promising to take care of me throughout the dismantling of brick upon brick so my heart could be revealed.

I felt naked and vulnerable, as He instructed me to face the emotions behind the hurt. When I faced them, the first year, I was looking at both my mother and my father. The following year, He would reveal the identity of my abusers.

Learning Forgiveness

No longer was I allowed to downplay how far the hurts of unresolved trauma really went. It was not about a verbal forgiveness, between them and me. It was a heart forgiveness, towards them. In fact, as the pain presented itself, I did not even know there were certain things I held against them.

This was deeper than our human relationships, and more about the spiritual lies that, over time, the devil had written on my heart.

He was calling me forward to come and sit at the cross, once again. He raised my chin up to look towards the face of my Savior, when the pain seemed unbearable, and completely out of control so I would not run from it. He even brought specific people alongside me, who would gently reside with me in His presence through the truth being revealed. No longer did He want me to bear those weights, and by forgiving them and binding the hurts into the cross, I released the hurt while also allowing Him entrance into another room in my heart, that it may be cleansed and set free.

With His promises of full restoration, I learned to trust He alone is my Shield and Protector.

It was easier for me to identify the forgiveness I had to give to my mother. Because of my dad's stroke, I did not realize how much I was harboring against him, alone, and both of them, collectively. Because I blamed her, repeatedly, and saw her as the cause for the changes, I had to forgive her for things she would never expect to need forgiveness for. Especially, because I had expected her to step into his place and fill the gaps.

It was painful to realize I had to forgive my daddy for choosing alcohol over me, for giving up on getting better, and for being unavailable. I had to forgive him for not saving me, and for not trying, in some way, to communicate with me instead of neglecting me. And these were just the tip of the iceberg. There was so much more that came with it, and as God would reveal it, I would voice that I forgive my mother and my father for this or for that. I just kept going until the waterfall of hurt just stopped and I wept, sorrowfully. In the dread of it, I was unable to breathe as I was acknowledging how I blindly resented the butchering of our family, but now these hurts and fears were being disarmed with honesty and love.

I had bound them to the cross, with a red ribbon, and it was finished.

I was allowed to rest in my Savior's love while He healed those hurts, took back the space I had given over to hatred, cleansed my heart, and replaced it all with pure love, while the darkness was commanded to give light to beauty.

The following year, He wanted me to forgive my abuser, and that made a little more sense to me. Although I was not aware of all that would entail, I would not realize the full effect of it until a week after I had returned home. One aspect that made it easier was my abuser, or perpetrator, did not have a face. All I remembered was someone else present, making my cousin and I perform these acts with each other. The sexual encounters changed over those four years from age six to nine, to include male interactions as well as female, but they were not as prevalent. My memories were still so disjointed and sporadic, not just concerning those instances, but my youth in general, due to the trauma of everything at once. I was thankful, as the offenses began rattling through my head, that they came quicker and easier than expected.

I had to forgive the perpetrator: For committing the sin against me,

For hurting me,

For the false beliefs,

For the lies,

For the belief that I was evil,

For the belief that I had caused it,

For feeling like the devil because of my memories,

For feeling like I had the power to transfer it,

For hiding,

For my same sex attraction,

For my destroyed relationships,

For unbroken promises,

For un-protection by my parents,

For the shame,

For the pain,

My Gift to God

For the homosexuality,

For the darkness,

For taking my innocence,

For the violation to my soul,

For what I perceived as my lost years,

For not being a mother,

For not being a wife sooner,

For the un-protection,

For the back turning,

For feeling like I had to be my own protector,

And, these were just to name a few.

The release and freedom I felt was outside of this galaxy, and I was relieved and thankful He had revealed these things to me. However, I did not know He was not finished with this yet.

Something else happened during that same week.

On the last night, while spending time in prayer and silence, I saw this picture in my mind of a girl with a bow and arrow. He began speaking to my heart about having authority and being used to accurately pierce the heart, like a warrior, with not only the arrow but with words. He said to me,

"I will speak,

You will listen,

I will give direct aim to the heart,

The arrow, and your words, will pierce straight through to the heart."

Not fifteen minutes later, one of the other team members came to pray with me and felt they had a word of encouragement to deliver to me, also. They said God wanted me to embrace the spirit of a warrior to fight for my brothers and sisters, for sons and daughters, for the church, for the truth, for generations to come and, to fight for love.

So, I left that week, feeling like a warrior!

I was ready, although I had no concept of what I was saying I was ready for!

All I could fathom was this was going to be the entrance into a ministry He wanted me to be a part of, and that I actually felt audaciously ready for.

That should have been my first clue that I, in fact, was not ready, because . . . I felt ready.

If ever there was a time I needed a finely tuned detector of God's voice and to be seated in prayer, it was at that very moment. Because He does not call someone, or place the spirit of a warrior upon you, without there also needing to be an air of humility that resides right along with it.

I would come to understand I did not know the definition of a warrior.

CHAPTER 21

Spirit of a Warrior

« —∞— »

"Warrior of My Heart, Lead Me, Teach Me Your Ways, Write Your Fight Song on my Heart that the Melody Echoed by my Steps are Yours Alone. Oh Lord, My Love, The Warrior of My Heart." Sarah McKinnis - Journal Entry

THE MEANING OF A WARRIOR conjures up many different images in the immediate mind, and what prompts in the forefront of mine has changed over the years. As a little girl, I thought a warrior was someone like my daddy, not afraid of anything and standing up for much. Then, life happened, and the image changed into a knight in shining armor, someone who would save me and take me to a nonexistent castle, never looking back. When that realization came collapsing into my lap, with a mountain full of disappointments and hurts, the image changed to something in fairy tales, not really a part of reality, but just in dreams. Thankfully, along the road, I did find out what a warrior was in Christ, and that verse in Exodus 14:14 "The Lord will fight for you, you only need be still," penetrated into the depths of my soul and the seed planted as a truth.

I did have a warrior!

I do have a warrior!

Then, my husband came along, and again, the dream of a warrior's protection was solidified in my daily life.

More recently, though, the meaning of a warrior has changed significantly!

Not only are warriors men, but they are women!

We fight in different ways, some on our knees, some in the battlefield, some in the spirit, some purely in love.

But, we fight!

And, we can win!

About four years ago, I attended a conference in which I came away feeling God calling me as a warrior, and I remember telling Him I was ready!

I was ready to pierce the hearts of many with truth and love. I was ready!

He had prepared me for the fight, and I was ready!

READY!

But then . . . true to God's form, what I was ready for was not what He had prepared me for. Yes, I was going into battle, but the battle I was facing was about to be a deep, deep . . . let me say this

Spirit of a Warrior

again . . . deep need for trust in Him to bring me into, and back out of, something I was going to have to fight for.

After flying back into Nashville from Kansas City, I was on a shuttle bus. On the phone, I had been talking with both my pastor and husband, explaining this fight and confidence I felt. Upon arriving at the shuttle drop off, Adam picked me up, and we traveled up the interstate, talking about everything more in depth, when we came upon a horrible accident. We could see an unrecognizable car wrapped around a bridge pillar. The accident had, apparently, just occurred as ambulances were pulling onto the scene while we drove slowly past. I remember praying for whoever was involved, and then turning back to conversation with my husband as we headed to meet our pastor and his wife for lunch before returning home. The confidence was overwhelming, and I voiced my desire to fulfill all I felt God calling me to, exuberantly.

And. Then.

We arrived back at our house and Adam turned on the television, just as the six o' clock news was beginning to air. I looked at the screen, heard the anchor talking about the wreck we passed, and then I saw it.

My cousin's name flashed across the screen.

Pictures of the crash.

Her Name.

The crash.

My Gift to God

Her Name.

The Crash.

I looked at my phone, no missed calls.

This must be a mistake. It happened hours ago, and they said she died at the scene; this just could not be. Shaking, I picked up the phone and dialed my aunt's number. Not my cousin's mother, but another aunt. She answered and all I could get out of my mouth was,

"Is it true?"

With confirmation, I was so upset that I found out from the news channel and not from my family. Then I sank into the floor as I realized I had been right there.

I was right beside her and had no idea as I prayed a simple prayer and then moved right back to what was important to me at the moment . . .

My calling . . . from God.

The confidence evaporated, and the disbelief set in.

The next few days were almost unbearable, and the arrows I had felt so sure in my spirit God had personally delivered into my hand, I laid them down, not caring where they were and with no desire to pick them up, ever again. But, the deepness was not over. At her funeral, we sat in the rain with umbrellas, and those of us close to her began to laugh. To onlookers, I am certain we all seemed crazy, but Breann loved the rain. As the sun was shining, we were sprinkled with a beautiful spring rain; it was just her style, and we couldn't help but acknowledge that she must be laughing at us.

I had no idea the fight was about to begin, as soon as I left that church.

The blame and fault enraptured my heart, all of the "what ifs" and "if only's" were deafening.

I knew I could not have saved her, not from the wreck or from any of the other things she had been facing personally, but still, the responsibility landed with solidarity. After several days of struggling with this, I went into the church for a day of prayer.

Alone, just me and God.

My spirit was inconsolable.

Something was breaking inside of me, and I knew I was in dire need of some help.

Along with the fault invading every crevice of my being, and having laid my arrows down, God was ripping open my heart and exposing it, laying it on the table, pumping, but not beating.

My fight was gone. With her death, came an onslaught of my childhood memories, and the sexual abuse that, for so many years, I could only remember certain details of. Although she had not been "the" cousin, that everything had happened with, she had told me she had knowledge of it. I do not know exactly what the trigger was, but while I was praying,

Flashbacks began, and they were leveling me.

My Gift to God

HELP!

I needed help!

My calm and caring husband, alongside our pastor and his beautiful wife entered into some deep, let me say again, deep inner healing prayer.

God took me back to this time in my life that was so imprinted on every decision I had ever made in life thereafter, exposed the enemy's lies, and revealed the truth to me.

It was torturous.

It hurt.

He took me there gently, surrounded by people who loved me, and then He ripped open the lies so my heart may have new life and fresh blood.

The truth was exposed, and although in the midst of it, I was literally vomiting, He was fighting for me.

My husband was fighting in prayer.

Kim was fighting in prayer.

Pastor Dale was fighting by leading me through what Jesus was showing me.

I needed only to be still and trust Him.

Hunkered over in the chair, clutching my stomach, tears streaming out of my eyes and snot out of my nose, while screams exited the depths of my soul, was exhausting.

Spirit of a Warrior

This picture of devastation, I know now, was beautiful to Him, because I was completely surrendered.

I had to be surrendered.

How else could I fight for Him, if I was not going to surrender all things to Him?

Even the hurt . . . especially the hurt.

What He revealed to me that day, in the depth of despair, was the identity of not only one, but two other people who shared space in that room. Whereas for so long, the memory had included only me and my cousin, now, I saw the other two faces. I heard their voices and the explicit instructions accompanied by daunting threats that became our directives for years upon years.

It connected the dots of the room I had just left from playing this game, censored by two others, to running frantically out of the house towards the barn, screaming and crying for my daddy, only to find he was not well and being whisked away. It also revealed the nature of another station of the abuse that had hurt me, internally, with physical male manipulation I had never recalled prior to this day.

But also, what was revealed in the screaming pain, that I was enduring all over again, was the fact that Jesus had been there in the room with me.

He had been shielding me from the identity of those perpetrators in protection, not just from the other traumatic events of that day, or the previous years.

My Gift to God

He needed it to be revealed, in His timing, and not in mine.

In those moments of inner healing and pain, He revealed the identities of these people and the truth to me. The difficult factor now was the reminder He had already had me forgive them less than two weeks prior.

Forgiveness is tricky when God leads you to do it, because what I knew was the forgiveness had been given innocently and authentically, based on what I knew to be true at the time. Which really was not much, compared to recent events, but it had been given and He was not going to allow me to take it back.

Even when I found out where they lived, and drove by their houses, alone,

I could not pull in the driveway.

I could only hear Him speaking to me, "This, is not what I intended."

These doors were not for me to knock on, nor were they were mine to open.

He had revealed to me the truth, so the devil could no longer meet me there. He, alone, my Father in Heaven, my Abba, who cares deeply for me, with no single detail being mistaken, would deliver justice and judgment appropriately. It was not mine for the taking.

I had to relinquish my power, and my desire for vengeance, to the One who trusted me enough to reveal the truth.

Spirit of a Warrior

To this day, He has allowed me to utter the names of those involved merely once, and although I have been asked by certain family members to expose them, the permission to do so has not been granted. Quite frankly, I do not know that it ever will be and I am peace with that, now.

I understand the intentions of wanting justice served. But, I know even greater, the heart of my Father is to have every heart return to him. Thus, I lay it back at the cross each time the desire to reap judgment creeps back into my mind, knowing the voice that delivers that to my ear does not have my best interest, or the interest of others, in their heart. But, I can tell you this sincerely, it was an extremely painful experience.

Do I ever want to do it again? No.

Would I do it again? Yes.

Will I do it again? Most likely.

The more hurt He heals, that we allow Him to heal, the deeper the fight.

That is why He called me a warrior.

He gave me the spirit of a warrior, deep within, not for myself, and not as a badge of honor.

He has called me to fight, with those who feel they cannot.

He has called me to fight, for those who will not fight.

To stand in a vast gap, even when others do not even see it.

My Gift to God

So, my image of a warrior has changed, once again. It may be with a bow in hand, it may be with heels and pearls on, but it is always with prayer. The spirit of a warrior resides within, with a depth in prayer on our knees, as well as standing beside, and for, one another. We must fight for each other, and lift each other up. We must not stay hunkered down in the depths of hurt that does not complete us, but release and surrender all of our desires, for protection and perfection, to the One who knows it all.

He calls us to fight, in the battlefield, and in our homes.

He calls us with strength, and He calls us with humility.

He calls us with Love, and He calls us with Spirit.

But He does call, and He calls ALL of US!!

Not just me, and not just the one who seems to have it all together, because, trust me that is one of the biggest lies.

None of us have it together, without Him, and I am tired of pretending that I do.

CHAPTER 22

Restoration

《 —∞— 》

Psalm 93 "The Lord reigns, he is robed in majesty; the Lord is robed in majesty and is armed with strength. The world is firmly established; it cannot be moved. Your throne was established long ago; you are from all eternity. The seas have lifted up, O Lord, the seas have lifted up their voice; the seas have lifted up their pounding waves. Mightier than the thunder of the great waters, mightier than the breakers of the sea- the Lord on high is mighty, your statutes stand firm; holiness adorns your house for endless days, O Lord."

AS I SIT HERE, ON THE porch of a bed and breakfast in Amelia Island, FL, listening to the wave's crash on the shore, it is not lost in my spirit or on my heart how mighty the ocean is. How powerful it is, and how much emotion it exudes in the depths of our souls just by hearing it, standing before it, or wading just as far as we dare go into it. What do we know of the ocean? We cannot fully measure its capacity of water around the globe, we cannot fully measure its absolute depth and what exists below a certain level, and we cannot fully measure its strength, the velocity with which it turns things to and fro. I love to deep-sea dive and see what is below, to the depths in which I am certified to go. There are many who relish the deeper depths and have done so, but in the utter darkness of the sea, still so many things are lost and not found or seen, beyond a certain level. How true this is in our Father's love for us!

Our Father in Heaven, who created the oceans and the stars.

Immeasurable "things," Immeasurable "capacities!"

How great is the Father's love for us?!

How mighty is the Creator of the Universe?!

While sitting here in the wee morning hours of September, I am reminded of how great His love is and how mighty He is. This is a weekend of further restoration in my life. I have experienced restoration in multiple, tangible, and intangible layers, over the past five years, but this weekend is a little different. He is revealing to me, not only what I allowed to be taken in my years of running, but also what he has given me throughout my life that I will no longer willingly give for anything this world holds.

Let me start here; it is easy to misunderstand the Ten Commandments, especially when it comes to honoring your father and your mother. This is more than simply loving them, as honoring your father and mother can take on many different facets. I am not going to go into a dissertation on what the Bible says about this, but rather share my experiences of how this was revealed in my journey to becoming a daughter in Christ's name. I have spoken, in previous

Restoration

chapters, about the loss of a relationship with both my parents, my father as a young girl and my mother over the period of many, many years. But, since giving myself fully to a relationship with my Abba, He has restored both of these with even greater mightiness than the ocean, and greater vastness than the skies!

This weekend, my momma and I are on a vacation, just the two of us. I cannot recall the last time we have done this, just her and I. I knew, going into this weekend, there would be a change, a revelation on my heart. We still have some time to go before the fulfillment of our trip, but already I am experiencing those revelations with a thankful heart. As I write, the morning sun is coming up on the horizon and a new dawn is rising in my relationship with my mother. A thankfulness and an appreciation, no longer dreading my time together with her, but rather anticipating our time. She is sixty-five years old as I write this, and it has been roughly five years since I allowed a true relationship with her to begin to develop.

We began this trip with a stop in Savannah, GA with its picturesque streets, lined with live oaks, dripping with Spanish moss, historic homes and buildings dating back to the 1700's, and river streets lined with cobble stones and bricks. Touring the city was at a slower than normal pace for me, as my mother has developed extreme arthritis in both knees. Taking her arm to help her along the streets added to the nostalgia of our trip.

My Gift to God

Although prior to this, I would have been impatient in being slowed down, the first of many revelations came tearing into my heart. I love my mother, and the years she would have been most vibrant were in the days I allowed the enemy to sequester me from the very woman who carried me in her womb, who birthed me, and then who raised me through very difficult circumstances. Ungrateful and unwilling to give in to anything because of blame and hatred, misunderstanding and hurt, lies and distorted memories written on my heart, I denied her access to her one, most precious, gift during the years in which she was most active and most invigorated. Stealing her joy became my mantra and offering up hurt, my goal. I wanted her to feel all of the pain I had experienced, so I dished it out as often and as boldly as possible, not caring what it would do to her.

The second revelation came in seeing what a giving and caring heart she has. As a nurse, this is not unexpected, but as a mom, I did not give her credit for that aspect of who she is. How I thank God that, no matter how many times I denied her, she never gave up on me, but instead continually gave me to God in prayer and supplication. She trusted the only One she knew she could, my Creator, the One who knit me together in her womb. The third revelation is how precious she is to me now, and how God is the restorer of truth, when we allow Him permission to do so, and we learn to trust that all things are possible through Christ!

Restoration

The restoration with my father has come incrementally over the last few years. It has been a transition from merely being his caregiver to seeing him as my earthly father, who still has so much to teach me when I allow him to. Somewhere between feeling like I had lost him at nine, to his presence being so jagged throughout my teen years, and then at eighteen being handed over his total care, I had morphed from a child into a parental role with no fruition of maturing taking place. I had to learn on the fly what to do and how to handle situations. Although I felt I had become pretty adept at taking care of things, they became just that. Taking care of things. Buying his groceries, paying his bills, filling out his insurance paperwork, or whatever else came up that needed to be taken care of. But, when God started speaking to me about this forgiveness stuff towards my daddy, it was a difficult pill to swallow.

There was never a doubt I loved my daddy, but where the lines were blurred was what I loved him for. Realizing I had never gotten past losing him at nine, and seeing him before me now, as alive and well, made me stop in my tracks. Taking into account all he still wanted to show me, and realizing he had also grieved the time he gave to alcohol instead of pouring that time into his daughter, I was also beginning to see that, although I desired true success in my career, I sometimes used it to gain the recognition I wanted so deeply from him. I wanted him to be proud of me, but my actions were not always very honorable. Some of the ways I had gained success

My Gift to God

would not have honored the name of my father, as I trampled on people to get there or did not care the pain I projected on relationships, all for the sake of money and success. These were not attributes my father would have taught me. Again, it was a lesson in humility. God was setting my heart right and teaching me to earn success through a good name and reputation that was pleasing in all man's sight, not just the limited vision I would present to my earthly father.

But, never would this thought my daddy still had so much to teach me, or that I longed for so much more time with him on this earth become more perceptible, than in the early morning hours of December 29, 2012.

It was a Saturday morning, and the clock on my phone read 5:58 a.m. I awoke with an urgency, as what had woken me up was hearing my daddy screaming my name! I awoke quickly and was confused because it sounded like he was in mine and Adam's bedroom, the scream had been so loud! I began screaming back,

"Daddy, Where are You?!"

This woke Adam up. I was searching the room, stumbling around in the dark trying to figure out where he was, because I was certain by the sound of things he had come over to our house from his cabin. But, he wasn't there, so I ran outside and when I got to him, he was barely whispering my name.

There had been no scream.

Restoration

The Holy Spirit had woken me up, and I knew it immediately!

Adam and I did a quick assessment and determined we needed to get to the hospital, and I was going to drive us there. Living out in the country has some advantages, but waiting on the nearest ambulance station, which was at least twenty minutes away, is not one. We both knew we had to move quickly. Adam helped get him to the car while I grabbed our belongings and insurance information, and off we went. I was booking it over a hundred miles an hour yelling at my daddy not to close his eyes and not go to sleep as he kept trying to nod off. Screaming prayers to God to, "Please, just get us there quickly and safely," but also telling God the hardest prayer that could be released, verbally, from my mouth.

I was telling God, "You know I love him so much God! But I know you love him even more than I do. You have promised me, for years you were going to heal my daddy and I don't know if that is going to be an earthly healing or a heavenly one, but I trust you God. I have to give him back to you, I have to trust you, because I don't know that I can handle this right now."

We pulled up to the emergency room and I was getting him out of the car, frantically trying to get someone to help me. They brought a wheelchair out, as he began vomiting. Immediately, they wheeled him down the hall while I explained his symptoms of arm pain and stomach pains, as well as nausea, while giving his medical history and they began to do an EKG. The doctor then asked if he

My Gift to God

had any prior heart problems, to which I answered, no and she said to me, "Well, he does now. He is having a heart attack and we are going to call Life Force to fly him to Erlanger Hospital in Chattanooga."

I thought my knees were going to buckle right under me.

The nurses reassured me, as the doctor made the call, that we had done everything right up until this point, driving him there instead of waiting, and moving quickly. They were equally surprised he was still awake, coherent, and attempting slightly to communicate with me.

He could not keep the aspirin or water down they gave him so they began an IV. It was not too much longer I heard the helicopter outside and the flight crew came rushing in. My daddy, being the calm man that he is, started whispering "Huey" softly to me, and twirling one of his fingers in the air while pointing to the flight nurse. He wanted me to tell them about his time in Vietnam, so I explained he had been a gunman in the helicopters during two tours of Vietnam and helicopters made him a little nervous, ever since. The head flight nurse took my sweet daddy by the hand and said, "Well, you are in good hands. Our pilot flew in Vietnam and will take good care of you."

With that I kissed my daddy on the head, as he looked at me with weak eyes and called me "Baby." And, out they went while telling me they would call me when they landed. The emergency room staff

Restoration

were truly amazing at how quickly they acted, and how reassuring they were. They had bundled the belongings we came in with, together, so I could leave promptly, after thanking them with tears streaming out of my eyes.

I rushed back out to the car and opened the door just as I heard the helicopter begin to take flight and I fell to my knees, right there beside the car.

Praying to God to please, please take care of my daddy!

I gathered myself back together, threw the belongings in the car and headed home to get Adam, who had stayed behind to close everything off and take care of things until he had word from me on what to do. That was the longest drive of my entire life. Longer than driving to and from Kansas City, longer than anything I could remember. I kept checking my phone, waiting on the flight nurse to call, and there was nothing.

Silence.

I called my mom, my Aunt Sherry, and the pastor and then just waited for my phone to ring.

Finally, the flight nurse called and said they had taken him back to surgery. He apologized it had taken awhile to call, but he explained there had been some complications during the flight, but he was in good hands, now. With directions on where to go when we arrived, he wished us well and told me he would check back in on us later, which he did several times.

My Gift to God

Once Adam and I found the tiny waiting room, it seemed another eternity of waiting began, accompanied once again, with this deafening silence. Pacing and praying was all I really knew to do. Adam was all too familiar with all of this, from when his dad had passed away, and was quietly praying and calming me as much as possible. My Aunt Sherry arrived, and then, not long after that, his Cardiologist came in the room and began telling me the brevity of the situation.

She was surprised he was still alive! That was comforting . . .

She then began asking me a lot of questions, because along with the heart problems, they had just found, his kidneys were in extreme distress. This was all news to me! He had overcome some medical issues the year we moved back to Tennessee, but no one had ever mentioned any of the things she explained. He had a massive heart attack that morning, with a one hundred percent blockage in his descending aorta, which is the main artery into the heart. He also had two other blockages. But, because of the severity of the one and, all that had been done while in surgery, they could only afford to place a stent in the main artery. He was too weak to continue, so they had to leave the others alone. Also, his kidneys were only functioning at nineteen percent, which was on the crest of kidney failure.

She leveled with me. The next forty-eight hours were critical. She explained the medicine he would be required to take from now

Restoration

on, to maintain what had been done in surgery and described what we were facing with his kidneys. She was breaking it down in realistic terms and, although that was what I wanted her to do, hearing all of this ripped my heart open.

I was not ready to lose my daddy.

The next week proved to be torturous, but also took me to another level of belief and faith as I watched miracle after miracle performed by God, right before my eyes. It was not lost on me that it was Him, and Him alone, taking care of my daddy. I was allowed to see him after surgery, before they took him to the Cardiac Care Unit (CCU), and he was still trying to reassure me he was okay, all while pointing his finger towards Heaven. He knew who was taking care of him, also.

It was amazing how full the critical care waiting room was. We found some seats in the corner, waiting for time to pass until we could visit him again. Although the room was large, I felt cramped and confined and began walking the halls outside of the CCU praying aloud. At first, I did not know what to pray, so I just started with the Lord's Prayer:

"Our Father, who art in Heaven, Hallowed be thy Name. Thy kingdom come, Thy will be done, on earth as it is in Heaven. Give us this day our daily bread, and forgive us our trespasses, as we forgive those who trespass against us. And lead us not into temptation, but deliver us from evil. For thine is the kingdom, and the power, and the glory, for ever and ever. Amen."

It was all I could get out of my mouth and I am so thankful that, over that week, there were so many people praying for us, and with us. There were many visits and phone calls, but if it had not been for Adam, and some of those closest to me, I really do not know how I could have made it.

I would not leave my daddy there, alone. What if something happened and no one was there? What if he was trying to communicate? He would get frustrated when no one, but the two of us, understood our own language and what he was trying to say. There were too many what ifs for me. So I stayed, and at night, when they turned off the lights in the waiting room, I tried to curl up on a pallet I had made, under some chairs, because all of the recliners were taken. When that would not bring rest, I walked the halls.

The very first night I came extremely close to being kicked out of the hospital for doing just this. Aunt Sherry had followed Adam home, to get some of my things, and brought them back down the same evening, including my Bible and a pillow. I began walking the halls, once again, at about one o'clock in the morning. I was just walking and praying, walking and praying, when two security officers barreled down the hallway towards me, marching in unison and with intention. They marched straight up to me and asked what I was doing, so I explained. After several minutes of questioning, they realized I was not a homeless person, although I am sure I looked like one because I had not changed clothes from that early morning drive with my daddy in the car. I did not appear intoxicated by drugs or alcohol, so they, kindly, asked me to go back to the waiting room. They also informed me they had a lot of trouble with people coming in that did not need to be there and, for my safety, I needed to stay in that locked waiting area. When I asked if there was somewhere I could pray, they were kind enough to lead me down a little hallway to a tiny chapel.

There was no heat in the room, so I went back to the waiting area, gathered my blanket, pillow, and Bible, and returned to lie down on the pew, to read and pray. There were two significant things that happened that evening. The first was God led me to read Psalm 56:3 "When I am afraid, I will trust in you." And, the second was when I got up to leave several hours later, standing outside of the chapel door was one of the security guards. He told me the doors to the chapel did not lock and he had wanted to make sure I stayed safe while inside.

God had sent me a watchmen because He knew I was scared. I learned that this gentleman had not left the entire time I was in the chapel. He told me he felt he needed to be there, and he had heard the concern in my voice, earlier. I was amazed and relieved. As the morning sun came gushing through the waiting room windows, I learned more about the doctor's concerns of a mass that could be

My Gift to God

cancerous. This was news on top of the kidney and heart problems that were already of grave distress. That verse, from the evening spent guarded in the chapel, became even more relevant to my heart. Each visit with another doctor, and with my daddy, seemed to bring on more and more questions. Later that afternoon, I was walking outside of the CCU once again, praying, when God reminded me of the verse and told me to lay every fear down before Him.

So, I began pacing again and started praying "God, when I am afraid of _____, I will trust in you." Inserted in the blank was each and every, little and big, fear.

When I am afraid, of losing my daddy, I will trust in you.

When I am afraid, of my daddy suffering, I will trust in you.

When I am afraid, of making the wrong decision, I will trust in you.

When I am afraid, of _____, I will trust in you.

The list seemed endless, at first. At one point, while I was walking and praying, his Cardiologist came around the corner. I did not want to bother her, but she stopped, of her own accord, and wanted to reassure me. She walked with me for five minutes although she did not have to do that. But, once again, God was providing answers to me quickly, knowing the condition of not only my daddy's heart, but also his daughter's. The entire week, I watched as I began praying specific prayers about questions to ask or for specific mile-markers to be accomplished, such as his blood pressure lowering or for the blood to leave his urine, among so many others. I would see them happen within hours. Incrementally, He was answering my prayers. It was truly amazing, but each prayer was a submission to God's will and not my own.

He was teaching me.

The acknowledgment that I was not ready for my daddy to be gone, because there was still so much I desired to learn from him, slipped into my mind. No longer did I want my daddy just because he was my daddy. I wanted to know him more fully.

All off those questions I had tried to get my mother to answer, back in my twenties when she would not desire to relive the past, I wanted to ask him. God was giving me the opportunity to not just be my daddy's caretaker, but to become his daughter, again. When my mother came down to help me get the house ready for him to come home, He would bring the three of us closer together.

He was no longer able to stay in his cabin, that Adam had built when we came back from Kansas City. Now, he was going to be in the house, with us. Adam had been busy, making a ramp and getting the spare room cleaned out for his homecoming. One week later, after he was released, Momma was with us to drive him home, help me clean out our cabinets, answer a million medical questions I had, and begin the process of changing our diets and cooking habits to coincide with all of these new medical conditions. Over the last two and half years, she has been there to celebrate, with me and daddy, each positive doctor's report of no cancer, kidney function increasing to almost sixty percent, which is considered normal, and improved cardiac functioning.

As a family, there has been reconciliation and restoration beyond my expectations. God is still doing His business, and everything is not perfect, by far, but He alone is leading the charge because the submission is to His will alone.

The depth, and the width, and the height that is our Heavenly Father's love for us is truly immeasurable and mighty. I have experienced it. I am experiencing it.

And, the awesome thing about His love is that it is exactly that way for each and every single one of His children.

All of His creation! He loves in that Way!

We cannot measure the vastness, the depth, or the velocity with which He loves us.

He is Mighty, yet Gentle!

If only we take the time to get to know Him.

CHAPTER 23

Encompassing Love
«—∞—»

AFTER THE SHIFT OF GOD pursuing me, I gained this hunger for Him, and our relationship changed significantly. No longer was He this God way off in the distance, waiting to thrash me with lightning every time I made a mistake, but He became the One I wanted to talk to about every little thing. Because He had proven Himself faithful in not letting the pains and hurt overtake me when they were revealed, I wanted to know more. I desired to trust Him more. I wanted to know what this thing in the Bible was about being Christ-like or Christ-minded.

What did it mean, exactly?

The more I asked, the more He began to show me.

He took me through the Ten Commandments, breaking them down and exposing to me how I had broken them all.

Now, you may say "She has not said anything about killing anyone so far!" and you would be correct.

Physically, I have not murdered anyone, but in my mind, my thoughts, and my words, as well as in my heart, I have.

My Gift to God

Again, we walked through a difficult season, but it was a long, gentle walk in which He was changing the nature of my heart, again with the truth, that our relationship would go deeper still. This was not a walk of shame or a dark walk of judgment; this was a walk towards the light, outside of the caverns of darkness I had been traipsing through for the majority of my life. Jesus was taking me on a journey through the dark corridors, extinguishing false beliefs, so our communion would become richer and more pure.

He took me straight through that list of commandments and with each acknowledgment of the exact stature of my heart, we went even deeper into communion and developed this authentic relationship with no secrets between Him and me.

I mean, He knew it all anyway, right?

But, the conversation made it real to me, and drew us closer together.

Lovingly, this is what He disclosed to me, through the Ten Commandments, of what the true condition of my heart was, what it had been and what He wanted me to learn:

1st Commandment - Love God - Have no other Gods before Me- I had many gods in my life (my mountains, my career, my success, money, things, control . . . etc.) and when the devil delivered the very intimate blow by Brian those years ago, I had completely turned my face from God, willingly and adamantly. I had walked away; more pointedly, I had run away. Instead of running to the One who would have taken that hurt and replaced it with truth and love, I did what I had always done. I relied on myself for protection and ran to escape, but what I had run into was a much harsher captivity, laced with lies and pain. I ran straight into the darkness, seeking any destruction I could find. My heart, mind, and eyes had been opened to things of this world I wish I could erase from my memory. But, they were mine to own. I had participated in these decisions because I was more confident in myself, than I was in anyone or anything else, especially Him. I did not think I needed Him, nor did I want Him. But then, He drew me back in, lovingly, and has turned the things I have seen and experienced into a spirit of discernment He wants used to spread unimaginable love, truth, and hope just as He has shown to me.

2nd Commandment - No Idols - I had many idols to deal with and to lay down. Money, adventure, my selfish wants and desires, pride and rebellion, to name a few. It had really just become all about what Sarah wanted and no one else. All of the attributes God had created me with, such as being adventurous and independent, had not been used to glorify God, but to glorify myself. This was not His intention, for me to take the instinctiveness of my DNA and use it for something to seek solace in, instead of understanding that He was the One who could and had led me out of all I had been through. My power of protection in no way matched His love and protection of me. No mountain or ocean was meant to replace Him, but rather for me to see Him in them. Without Him, they are powerless. By coming to rely on Him for provision in all things, whether that was physically, emotionally, mentally or materially, He has shown me it is not at all about what I do, or how well I do it. He has all of our best interests at heart, always, and trusting in that is all we need to do. It is all I needed to do.

3rd Commandment - Do Not take the Lord's name in vain . . . This commandment had less to do with my language and much to do with my actions. I had proclaimed Christianity and that I was a Christian since I was a little girl, but my actions in no way reflected that. Not only did my actions not reflect that covenant with my Father in Heaven, neither did my thoughts or words signify this. Being a Christian is something I not only had taken lightly throughout my life, but I had used when it was convenient for me. Using it, whether it was to place myself in a better position than another person or to have someone view me in a certain light, with no regards to what I was really professing when I called myself a Christian. The commandments were simply a chapter in the Bible, in which I really did not take beyond the surface level of the words. He was revealing to me this was so much deeper than not cussing and using His name in vain. He wanted my actions to match my words and that meant loving and being honorable. Taking what Jesus had experienced on the cross to heart, and not just as a story in the Bible, understanding the cost of my redemption and with that understanding, a reverence replaced my flippancy towards being a Christian.

4th Commandment - Keep the Sabbath Holy - Desecration of the Sabbath day was easy for me. I had no day set aside for the Lord. I had a day that I would go to church to ask for superficial forgiveness before heading back out into my day to do whatever I had already planned before I ever darkened the doors of the church. My weeks, when I had attended church regularly, were still not about serving the Lord. They were about doing whatever I wanted, knowing on Sunday I could go back and ask for forgiveness, and He would give it to me. Because that's what the Bible said, right? Ask and Ye shall receive! That had been my mindset. Church was my get out of jail free card once a week, that and to be seen, but that's not what He was after. He was showing me the Sabbath carried on much further than one Sunday morning a week. And, forgiveness was not something to be used at my will, as I desired. True forgiveness is actually a stature of the heart that is then reflected externally. Keeping the Sabbath was not about "Going to Church," but, rather, about coming to know this family He had called me to be a part of. To understand there was an inheritance at stake, not just going to Heaven or going to Hell. Keeping the Sabbath holy is about coming into communion and this one-on-one relationship that He desires from each of His children. He still continues to call me deeper, just as He does with all of us.

My Gift to God

5th Commandment - Honor Thy Father and Thy Mother - I think we already covered this one, but this one was, again, deeper than just obeying them. He wants us to honor our parents, just as we strive to bring Him glory, in our thoughts and words and actions that are representations of our heritage. And even though there are many of us whose heritages seemed to be defiled throughout our lives, He does not call us to lift up the ungodly actions of others, but to be good representations as children who understand that listening, heeding, and submitting to the authority of our parents will teach us honor and respect to other levels of authority throughout our lives. We may think that we have it all together, and can take care of ourselves due to certain circumstances. He does not desire for His children to not understand maturity and respect, and without learning that father/child relationship, how can we ultimately understand the levels with which He wants to teach us things? I was lucky that, in the absence of real parental authority that I could hold onto, He kept interjecting people into my life to carry those roles and teach me things. He does not leave us, nor does He forsake us, especially as young children. When there is a lack of what His ultimate design is for the family, if we look back, we can find the people interjected in our lives and how He provided for us all along. He showed me, in the love and concern that had been there, in order that when it came time for Him to really teach me about honoring my father and mother, I would recognize His hand.

Encompassing Love

6th Commandment-Shall not Murder - As I said before, my thoughts and my heart had killed many a soul, not just in wanting some people dead, but in stealing their happiness and wanting to inflict pain, all for my protection. I had a deep-seated hatred against my mother, for sure, but also for others. He showed me by harboring the hatred, internally, I would never understand the true capacity for love in my own heart. My barriers would remain up, to protect myself by holding onto these things, and by hating, I was inflicting a pain that was not suitable in the eyes of my Father. He did not create me with hate. It was something I had learned. When He lovingly revealed the roots of truth to me, He alone was able to replace the hurts that turned into hate with a compassion only He has to give. My peace, in Him, no longer had room for these darkened spaces that had projected disdain for so many. His desire was to look into my heart for the truth and show me how He would have me handle the difficult moments of my life, not with hate, but rather with love and truth.

7th Commandment-Shall not Commit Adultery - I had committed this, in deed and in thought, throughout my life. Not in my marriage, but I broke this commandment in those times when my decisions were influenced only by my happiness, without concern for others. There were some people I dated who would have considered us to be in a relationship, whereas I merely viewed them as pawns in my game of happiness and adventure. You may read this and say, "It does not apply because you were living in the homosexual lifestyle," but, to me, it applies. These were relationships and not to be disregarded. It does not matter whether I was dating women or men, I was still playing with God's children. I had no chastity in body, mind, or words. I did not seek a purity or understand the depths of self-control until God revealed the truth of what a covenant meant to Him. This is one of the reasons the letter I wrote to Adam, and had given to him prior to us taking our vows, was so important. This marriage was more than being merely about a sexual relationship, but more importantly about coming into communion with my husband, purely, with God at the forefront of our relationship. My submission to him as head of our home was an endearment of respect, which ultimately shows my love. I have tasted things of this world, seen and participated in vile acts that only my God can now censor from my mind and heart, and He does so, lovingly. Part of being so open and raw about my testimony has to do with this commandment as well. Where light is shown, darkness cannot prevail. I am honest, open and raw about these things so when the enemy or the devil, or Satan, or whatever you want to call him, begins to dangle things in front of me, tickles my ears with condemnation or presents opportunities from my past before me, I can say with authority, "Get behind me Satan!" Because committing adultery is so much more than the physical act, it is the very fabric Satan uses to rip us all open and tear apart the relationships, not just with husband and wife, but with Him, as well as families. Satan tempts our minds and bodies into seeking sexual fulfillment in avenues that are not his creation. When he can accomplish that and get to us in the secret places where we want no one to know about them, his clutches are more restraining than the handcuffs I wore when I was arrested. He attempts to arrest us and hold this condemnation over us when all our Heavenly Father and Abba wants to do is say, "Just give it to me and I will take care of it all. Just trust me." It may hurt to be exposed at first, but the pain is nothing compared to the joy in the morning from the release. No longer does that voice that seeks destruction have credence over God's.

8th Commandment - Shall not steal - Again, I had committed this in deed, as well as in thought, and by stealing intangibles such as joy and happiness and time with my mother, just to name a few, I had participated in stealing so much more. I felt I had the authority to withhold things that did not belong to me and not only was this robbing others, but I was also robbing myself. By not fully understanding how faithful God had been to me, and how I never returned the favor, I was robbing even from Him. He had created me with so many characteristics I used against Him. So much provision had been showered over me, physically and monetarily, yet tithing or using the gifts He created me with were not thought of, at all. Stealing was more than just taking things, it was not being faithful with what was given. He opened my eyes to what giving meant and, also, what giving Him authority over all things meant. Whether that was time, talents, possessions, finances, relationships, or just being willing to trust Him with it all so He could prove His faithfulness, once again, by not reserving any area from Him.

9th Commandment - Shall not Lie or Bear False Witness - This was another tough one because, again, this was not just about words, this was an internal heart condition. Sometimes it is so much easier for words that tear people down to come out of our mouths than to take a minute and realize when we speak something, we are accountable for every single word from our lips. Whether the person is standing in front of us or not. But when we allow God into this area of our thoughts and our hearts, He is the only one with the ability and power to release us from them. I have spoken mistruths about others, or told certain stories with just the right twist on them that others may view someone in a particular light, based on those words. I have had to ask forgiveness from many a person for words of disdain against them. It is not always easy, but if we are to call ourselves Christians, we must remember what we are yoking ourselves with and that is to reflect the character of Christ.

10th Commandment - Shall Not Covet - Oh, the things I have desired that were not mine throughout my life, including a different family, as well as physical and material things that were not mine to own. But, once again, He was going to show me this was deeper than the physical. This was about learning to trust God with what He would provide us with, and not by any merit of my own. Learning to displace a covetous and envious heart, in order that it could be replaced with contentment and happiness with God's will and provisions, alone. He wanted me to learn the true meaning of trust through this conversation and this was probably one of the more painful ones, especially because not long after Adam and I had married, we experienced our first miscarriage. This would be the first of five we have suffered to date. And if you think a woman who has a longing for children, but for whatever reason cannot carry her own, should just get over it, I am here to tell you there is a lot more to it than that. Because, yes, there are children who need adopting or fostered or any other number of avenues to have a child or children in your home. But, it is not until God is allowed into that deep hurtful feeling of unworthiness, that a covetous and envious heart for all of the women walking around with pregnant bellies in our faces, or toting around two or three kids with the statement that, "We just don't want to have anymore" can be replaced with a heart of contentment for God's will. This has been a long, arduous journey for God to reveal to both Adam and I that, number one, the idea that this is a consequence of my past is not rooted in truth. Secondly, He has created in us a parental heart for a reason, and that is truth. He has shown us that we will be reunited with our babies dancing in Heaven, but, in the meantime, He is showing us how to parent His children without one under our roof. That does not mean that will not change and, one day, we may have a child or children in our home. But, we have come to this place collectively relying on the Radical God that we serve. We have both seen Him do so many miraculous things and I cannot wait to see more! What replaces the envy is expecting the radical, come what may, as long as it is His will and not one that we make happen. We have seen Him fulfill desire after desire that was, inexplicably, His hand. He has delivered even more than we thought we truly desired also, such as buying a farm, an increase in financial blessing that has allowed us to help others, as we have been helped, because He calls us to be faithful, and these are just a few of the things we have witnessed Him do. He does not give us a desire without a plan to have it fulfilled, and we know this intimately, so being content in His works is the most peaceful place I have ever resided in and one I wish I had learned a long time ago.

After God took me through each of these commandments that had been delivered, personally, to Moses on the Mountain, He just continued to unravel my heart to His love and to His promises. Never has He left His promises unfulfilled. They had been there all along and they are still there today!

It astounds me!

I mean, isn't it amazing that we cannot comprise His love for us in earthly measurements?

Encompassing Love

That our minds cannot begin to comprehend that He has no beginning nor no end to the depths that He will go for us?

That He is mightier than anything that has ever come against us?

He is powerful and He is mighty!

Let me say it again, He is Powerful and He is Mighty!

The depths of His love immeasurable, the capacity immeasurable, the velocity and strength immeasurable!

His love is like the ocean, mighty and immeasurable!

Physicists may argue with me and that is fine with me. But, put them on a little raft in the middle of the Atlantic Ocean with nothing in sight and leave them, then let them tell me how mighty they believe the ocean to be and how easily it can be measured. Reality is different than a lab and I have experienced the life aspect of His saving grace, of His outpouring of mercy, of His mightiness in my life to not only save me, but to restore me.

The key to it was that I had to be willing!

I had to learn to trust that, although I had to face some very difficult realities of my life and understand the consequences of my own freewill, He would restore me, lovingly, to all that was taken, as well as reveal what I had been given.

Do you know the cool thing about God?

He did not leave me there in those realizations because there was more to show me, and there continues to be more to reveal every single day. He is never done with us and I am more thankful for that

My Gift to God

today than yesterday, and definitely more thankful than the day He sat me in the chair to open my Bible and see the truth before me.

After leading me through the commandments to show me the stature of my heart, He then moved me on to do an in depth study of the book of Ezekiel. This became very interesting to me because it is such a misunderstood book in the bible. Many people, myself included, have thought this book was just laced with prophecies of judgment against nations, and crazy actions by Ezekiel, but it is so much more than that. There is a teaching I have included my notes to in the Appendix of this book, but there are some promises in Ezekiel that I want to take a step further with you, here. I am not covering the entire teaching, just the simple promise of restoration God began to show me in the beginning.

He revealed not only was He calling me to an obstinate and stubborn people, Ezekiel 2:2, but that the words would be delivered in truth, but also full of love. If you take the time to study the book of Ezekiel, you will learn at the root of it is a Father's outcry for His children to return to Him, just as He had cried out for me. His heart is for us all to return and His heart is, also, to shower each of us with this encompassing love so full that is unimaginable.

His call to us is in Ezekiel 18:30-32. "Therefore, O house of Israel, I will judge you, each one according to his ways, declares the Sovereign Lord. Repent! Turn away from all your offenses; then sin will not be your downfall. Rid yourselves of all the offenses you have committed, and get a new heart and a new spirit. Why will you die, O house of Israel? For I take no pleasure in the death of anyone, declares the Sovereign Lord. Repent and Live!"

Did you catch all of that?

It is not about Him judging us.

It is Him begging for us to turn away and to repent that we may have life. And, the two exclamation points, they do not come after "I will judge you," they come after "Repent, and Repent and live!" He calls out to each of His children, if only we hear the cry.

But, He does not stop there.

The call, after repentance, was to get a new heart and a new spirit and if you turn to look at Ezekiel 36:25-27, you will find the promises of the Lord, our God, on how this will be accomplished:

"I will sprinkle clean water on you, and you will be clean; I will cleanse you from all impurities and from all your idols. I will give you a new heart and put a new spirit in you: I will remove from you your heart of stone and give you a heart of flesh. And I will put my Spirit in you and move you to follow my decrees and be careful to keep my laws."

He tells us in those very promises, after crying out to us, that it is not all up to us. We just have to be willing to turn away and let His truths be established in our hearts, through truth and love. This is exactly what He did for me. He did not beat me over the head with the Bible or put a judgmental finger in my face. He said, "Come to me, sit and let me show you the truth, walk with me through the valleys of your life so that those places may be reestablished and your heart will know the truth, and then I will build a new Spirit inside of you."

I am not the same person I was five years ago, and I hope, in five more years, I can look back on today and say the same thing.

Because I want more!

I want more revelation and more truth, but I no longer want it, selfishly, for me.

CHAPTER 24

Love Thy Neighbor

《 —∞— 》

"God loves you unconditionally, as you are, not as you should be, because nobody is as they should be." – Brennan Manning

GOSH, HOW MUCH MORE SIMPLE can it get than that statement?

It is one of the most simple, yet profound, truths I have ever heard or read. If you do not know who Brennan Manning, or Rich Mullins is, I encourage you to read the book *The Ragamuffin Gospel* by Manning, or watch the movie *Ragamuffin* that is a story of the life of Rich Mullins and the effect Manning had on his life. In fact, you can YouTube some sermons of the late Brennan Manning that are incredible, and have drastically impacted my viewpoint of life on this earth as a Christian, and what that really means, to not just Love God but to Love thy Neighbor, as you love yourself.

After my journey through the Ten Commandments and Ezekiel, God began talking to me about Jesus coming to this earth to tear the veil and fulfill the Levitical laws of the church, and to leave us with the two greatest commandments of all:

1. Love God
2. Love Your Neighbor, As You Love Yourself

This world and the people in it, not excluding myself, deliver hurts to people on silver platters, as if they are delicacies, and it is everywhere we turn. My heart desires everyone to know they do not have to hurt or be hurt. I know God does not want us walking around in all of this pain, suppressing emotions until they explode in multiple ways, but there is only one way to overcome, and that is through the two greatest commandments that Jesus left us with. To love God and to love our neighbor as we love ourselves. I know that is challenging, because there have been times God has called me to love someone, in particular, that I just really did not want to. I ask Him, "Why do I have to do this?" But, He really does have a plan and, more often than not, when I challenge Him or ask repeatedly, why, it is usually because He wants to stretch me, and show me just one more layer of that love-onion.

And that is exactly what He was doing by walking me through the commandments, revealing this other level of love and truth, not in judgment, but so He could facilitate a change in my heart. He was doing just as He had said He would do in Ezekiel. He was giving me a new heart and a putting in me a new spirit, one that would understand what it was like to desire to be Christ-like or Christ-minded, with humility and love at the core of my being. By breaking me, He was building me up and making me new, again.

This is where the truth of the matter came out. He had been showing Himself to me in the purest form of love, so He may teach me how to love others, as I love myself, and what the implications of that are. To love your neighbor as yourself, there can be no secrets or hidden agendas.

Every single time I happen to hear the news, it overpowers me how much more love we need in this world, and how rampant hate is filling the mouths of those who say they are speaking in love, or doing things out of love. I just pray how long, sweet Jesus, do we have? Some days, I wish He would come on back and there are other days I am praying He waits a little longer because there are so many who are hurting and need to know Him. So, sometimes, it makes me feel selfish to say, "Come on back," just because of what I may be experiencing at the moment, when I know there are still so many of us, so many of His children, He wishes would return to Him. In fact, He wishes for all of us to turn our hearts towards Him. Knowing I am nowhere remotely close to perfect, I do that daily, I have to do that daily; I turn my heart to Him.

For the past several years, I have taken some time towards the end of December, to pray for the coming year. Each time I have done this, Jesus has met me in undeniable ways and has given me a picture that ends up being a representation for the coming year. The one for this year, 2015, really set me still and, as has happened other years, I am only seeing parts of it, so far. But, by the end of the year, I will see it fully, what He was showing me. This is a description of what He was showing me for the year of writing this book:

I was in a courtyard of an old city. I was knelt down beside a very large bundle of fruit and as people were walking by on the cobblestoned streets, I was attempting to use a paring knife to cut some fruit off the vines. But, I was having great difficulty and then a man walks up to me and I look up into the magnificent face of Jesus as He extends His hand for me to give him my paring knife. I hand it to Him and He says to me, "Let me show you how to cut the fruit." With that, the knife I was using turns into a machete, and He swiftly cuts the fruit off into my hand, to extend to those around me.

Several days later, in more prayer time for the coming year, He delivered to my heart instructions and they were to love God and to Love Your Neighbor, as you love yourself.

So simple, and right before us in the word of God, but how complicated that we do not even know, ourselves, how to be loved. So, how is it possible to extend this pure love Jesus came to this earth to show us? Instead of handing people banners for them to wave and pronouncing or marking them as this thing or that thing, we should be handing out the only fruit we have to give and that is the fruit of love from the Father. Extending the only true banner any of us should wave and that is that we are His Child.

Love Thy Neighbor

All of Us.

We are All His Children.

Not just you and me, or the person we sit beside in church or that we clasp hands and pray for, but everyone who was created in their mother's womb.

We each belong to Him.

And, He loves each of us. He loves all of us, equally and unconditionally. Oh, to know the Love of our Father and how to give the Love He gives to us.

I get asked a lot of times after sharing my testimony; what is it that someone should do or say to their daughter or son or friend or loved one that is homosexual?

I tell them the only truth I know to give them.

There is nothing you can say, or do, to or for them.

It has to start with our own hearts.

Prayers.

It starts with prayers.

The Truth is in the Word of God.

There is nothing anyone can say or do to the homosexual, or the murderer, or the thief, or the adulterer, or any other sin that can be accomplished without the love of our Heavenly Father. To learn to love purely, it has to come from the heart change. We are inundated with the enemy's trickery all around us, speaking of tolerance and injustice, when, at the core, what all of us needs is love.

My Gift to God

So that is what I intend to do, just as I was instructed -to Love You right where you are, because that is what Christ did for me.

He did not try to fix me; He just met me.

He stayed right there beside me, through all of the difficult things, while we established a relationship based on love and trust, and as we have kept walking, my heart has changed.

My eyes have changed. My mind has changed.

And, because of that, He has stirred up, in me, this desire to seek pure authentic relationships built on love, truth, and trust, just as Jesus has shown me.

He was writing on my heart this passion that resides, in me, today, at the very core of me, that seeks for Each and Every Person on Earth to know that no matter what they have done, where they are at, or where they have been, that they are FIRST and FOREMOST a SON or DAUGHTER of the MOST HIGH KING!

For everyone, all of His children, to come to know that He does not want you to come to Him as you should be, but that He desires for you to come just as you are!

The complicated, ugly, mess . . . that is how He wants us all to come to Him!

His question to us is simply this:

Are you willing?

Are you willing to give the only gift that God wants for us to give Him? Are you willing?

MY GIFT TO GOD
Written by: Sarah McKinnis

I am going to share with you a story that God laid on my heart several years ago. As you read this, I have two simple requests:
1. Will you picture the person in the story as yourself? 2. As you finish reading, will you seek the heart of your Father, for His child, in prayer?

Coming to God as this perfect, pretty, tidy, good little package: Perfect wrapping paper, Perfect pretty little bow, No creases in the paper, Nothing out of place. Presented as the Perfect Gift to God.

This is what I thought I had to do for so many years. Even though I grew up in the church, grew up with God represented and talked about, I still felt that I could not come to God unless I looked like that pretty little present. Perfect on the outside, Perfect on the inside. And then, I would be accepted.

Accepted into the kingdom of God, Accepted by the church, Accepted by society, my friends, coworkers, strangers. I had to walk a certain way, talk a certain way, and dress a certain way. But, these are all outward appearances . . . the internal reality of me . . . the real me...although I could dress my outside to be the perfect package, my internal reality was a mess . . . dirty and complicated!

Jesus met me, one day, while I was wrapping my gift once again. You see, I was constantly going through these cycles of "Being Good." At those times, I knew I could take off the wrapping that was over time being torn apart and I would rewrap it, all pretty and perfect and go back to God,

My Gift to God

giving my gift of perfection. But, Jesus met me one day when my package was completely destroyed and beaten up. I was attempting to wrap it all once again. But my faith was destroyed, I felt worthless, I felt discouraged...broken down . . . alone . . . and I was on the brink of giving it all up, no longer fighting the depths of despair.

This is where Jesus met me . . . Jesus met me right there and said, "Come . . . take a short walk with me." Not certain that I could even stand, he took me by the hand, led me down a short path and there . . . on the hilltop was this plain, wooden cross. It stood, majestic and mighty . . . weathered and beaten by the storms . . . but still it stood. Jesus helped me climb the hill, when I would stop . . . seemingly anxious and out of breath, He would nourish me and he would encourage me. Three final footsteps after climbing the hill, I was face to face with the cross.

I stood in awe and disbelief . . . not knowing whether to kneel, stand, fall down on my face, or run. Then Jesus handed me a box. It was my box . . . the one I had been attempting to rewrap . . . the one that was beaten up, bruised, looking ragged, and destroyed . . . He began telling me that I could sit it down at the foot of the cross, that I could give it all . . . every bit of it, to my Father in Heaven and never again would I have to rewrap it. He explained that it was up to me to give it all to God. I stood in disbelief and wonderment with all of the "what if's" and "but's" running through my mind.

Jesus asked me, then, to kneel down, still holding my battered box. So I knelt with Him . . . He spoke softly, "Sarah, don't you see. . . that this box, all beaten up and broken is the very most precious gift you could ever give to your Father? All of these things that are in your box, they are your life . . . No longer do you have to dress it up or try to hide it or give it away.

My Gift to God

Your Father, who art in Heaven . . . loves you exactly as you are . . . You are perfect to Him, just as you are. He has loved you from the beginning of time. He knitted you together in your mother's womb, already knowing your journey in life. Here . . . right here . . . He waits for this beautiful gift. It is up to you now, but I do have one final promise for you . . . When you choose to give him your gift . . . do not be afraid for He will shower you with Grace . . . Mercy will rain over you from the heavens, and He will wrap you in His eternal love . . . gentle, but mighty . . ."

I cried out, "God, Help Me, Please Forgive Me, Father . . . Here is this so called gift that is full of the foolishness of my life. I am so sorry, I am so . . . ashamed. I have hurt so many people Father, I have been disobedient. I have lied, and I have intentionally stolen the joy of others . . . So many things I have chosen and done God . . . WHY . . . WHY DO YOU STILL LOVE ME???"

And, in a very gentle voice . . . I heard, "Because you are my daughter."

I could no longer hold the box and the promise Jesus spoke began . . .

The grace, mercy, and love began demolishing the hurt, shame, and fear . . . The love, compassion, and gentleness was overwhelming!!!

So, I tell you . . . that whatever may be in your box . . . it is a gift!

You are a daughter. You are a son of the Most High King!!! He waits for you to give him the most precious of gifts . . . your heart, your life . . . your hurt, your pain . . . your shame, your grief. . . your sadness and your happiness . . .

I just have one question for you today . . .

Are you willing?

A Note from Adam

I HAVE HAD THE PRIVILEGE OF LIVING what I would call a rather quiet life, and I have enjoyed it. However, I do realize I may never understand the saving attributes of Christ in the ways that Sarah and countless others have.

When you hear someone like Sarah, tell how the miracle working hand of God reached into their lives in such a dramatic way that it sets their entire existence on a different course, and see the change that has taken place in their eyes and candor, it makes me jealous. And, indeed, it should provoke us to want to experience the limitless grace and mercy of Christ ourselves.

I always hear the same thing after Sarah gives her testimony, "What a strong husband you are to bear these burdens with your wife." I wish that were true. The fact is I fall every day, I doubt the reality of Jesus every day, I question His forgiveness, and His spirit. This one thing I know, that everyone is equal in His eyes. Equally destitute. Everyone. You cannot run from His presence, or His power. In fact, it is arrogance to even make plans for tomorrow.

I am a hard man, an exacting man. I have many vices, and generally the first thought that passes through my mind on any particular matter is definitely of the flesh and not of the Spirit. The Bible says the heart is deceitful and desperately wicked. I can attest to that, BUT there is something inside of me that constantly cries out for Jesus. It's like labor pains waiting for the birth, which is the revelation of all that He is to shine in my soul, It is how one responds to those labor pains that makes the difference.

My Gift to God

This is how I bear those burdens with Sarah.

First, I realize that if it were not for the immense grace of Jesus, I could have been, or could be any of those people in her past. Make no mistake about it, there is a war for your very soul. Evil is just a decision a way. The adversary knows what makes you tick and knows when you are weak.

Secondly, I realize that sin is the same across the board. I want my Lord to forget my sins. Therefore, it is my duty to forget others sins.

My prayer for you, the reader, is this: that on every page you see Christ, and that if you have not put your Faith in Him, that the thought of Him will invade every part of existence until you do. And, that you come to see that prayer, even when you don't know someone is praying for you, is the very thing that keeps you from being sifted like wheat.

My call to you, is to pray for someone and do not stop.

~ Adam ~

Acknowledgments

I CANNOT THANK ANY ONE person until acknowledging that this story, is God's story. His unending grace, love and truth is the fabric that is intertwined throughout my life, woven so intricately that the design is unmistakably written with His signature, everywhere.

To my Father, my Creator, my Abba, You are the sustenance with which I place one foot in front of the other. Discovering characteristics I never understood you could possess and knowing that I truly can "trust you without borders" and look forward to you taking me "deeper than my faith could ever wander." I am your beloved and you are mine, for eternity.

My Adam, the one who knows me fully, yet loves me anyway. Your honest, simple stature towards life is what drew me to you, but the complexity of your authentic love for Christ is what draws adoration from my heart each moment I look into your eyes. Your humbleness and fearlessness in always speaking the truth sets my soul alive and I thank you for standing beside me, as my truth is revealed to others. You have allowed not only for me to be vulnerable, but you, also, through exposing the ugly beauty of this story. Without you, this would not be possible.

To my Momma and Daddy, I love you! I thank God that He chose you as my parents, daily! Though the journey has been arduous and sometimes lonely for us all, you are both irreplaceable and treasured. I will always be, your little girl, your baby.

My Gift to God

James and Wanda, for opening your home and your hearts to me as spiritual parents, I love you! Your humbleness and unwillingness to never give up on God's will travels with me throughout this walk with God, and has taught me to always seek my Father's heart, first, in all things.

Clarence, Ruth and Carol Lea. A lifetime of knowing each other and an eternity to look forward to. Thank you for the fights, for the lectures, for the fun and the love. But most of all, thank you for the prayers, your obedience and the truth. Undeniably, you are my family, and without our time together, I am unsure of how this story would have turned. Deeply, I love you!

Stan and Kathay, for always loving me first. For talks and chocolate milkshakes and letting me read the paper in your living room. Your impact is limitless and will never be forgotten. I am glad that I am your second daughter. I love My Mr. and Mrs. P.

Brenda, you broadened my horizons of not only this world, but in how to love others selflessly, sharing all that you have and asking nothing in return. I love you unconditionally.

Vonda and Randy, I thank you for being more than just family! Your love and support is honest and selfless, I love you both!

Sherry, for not being afraid to ask the difficult questions, but also for being vulnerable yourself. I love you dearly!

Acknowledgements

For my family and those who have influenced my life along the way, I undoubtedly will forget to mention someone, so I want each of you to know how grateful I am for your support, and for affording me the opportunity to bare my soul to any who may choose to read this story. You are loved beyond measure.

Caritas, my sweetie and one of the best friends a person could ask for. You have had a seat for the show through so many important parts of my life, I am just thankful your love and friendship has always been waiting in the wings. You really are the wind beneath my wings and I love you.

Andrea, you have and always will be special. There are no words. I love you.

My sisters, you know who you are. We are a unique group with a fierceness towards and for each other that keeps me on my toes and I look forward to growing old with you all. Many prayers, much laughter, and love like no other.

Jeff, for never knowing what was next, but never being surprised. I adore our easy friendship.

Dale and Kim, for your friendship, love, support and prayers. My words do not satisfy what my heart wishes to express. Simply put, thank you.

Miss Sylvia, for your friendship, laughter and honesty. I truly cherish you and am thankful you and Ed allowed me a reprieve, at your cabin in the

My Gift to God

woods, to complete this book. I look forward to many more chapters with you!

Rebecca, gosh, where do I begin? I am thankful that you are not just my editor, but my friend and sister in Christ. Your honest feedback and consistent expansion of my thought processes and nudging boundaries was evidently ordained. Thank you for keeping me on course, I appreciate you!

Pastor John Brown, Pastor Gary Sears, Pastor Michael Obi, Pastor Teresa Norman, without your humble approach to sharing the love of Christ, this daughter may never have understood the truth.

Desert Stream Ministries, Andy, Annette, Dean and Ann, for leading me into a depth of communion never experienced before and modeling honest exposure of our most intimate thoughts and beliefs. You are the real deal, and I thank you for your integrity and your love for others!

Walter, Elita, Olga, Toby, Dave, Rebecca, Peter and Oleg, this group is what church is all about. I love you my brothers and sisters.

Lisa B. your quiet encouragement exceeds any friendship I have ever known. Thank you for the phone calls, the tea and the walks. You know what being a true friend is all about and I love you for that.

AC, for answering countless questions and providing clarity in the fog of this crazy process, I appreciate you immensely.

Acknowledgements

Sarah C, MickiAnn, Arlyne, Evie, God surrounded me with you lovely matrons to dress me, to encourage me, to pray for me, and to present me to my Father as a daughter. Thank you for ensuring I felt beautiful in the ugliness. Thank you each for your humble, honesty, but most of all thank you for your tears and your laughter. I love each of you.

And finally, to the readers, thank you. Please know that I love you, also and pray for each of you, daily, even if I do not know your name.

~ Notes ~

Teaching on Love through Ezekiel
Discourse by: Sarah McKinnis

I. The Book of Ezekiel: The first emotion seen is one of wrath and judgment, but the source of the emotion comes from God's heart, which is full of love. In our human actions, when we are angry, more often than not, it roots from a hurt. When your heart is hurt, you tend to do one of two things 1) mourn 2) get angry.

II. God does not forget His Covenant, even though there are consequences for our choices. He makes ATONEMENT!! Ezekiel 16:8 "... *I spread the corner of my garment over you and covered your nakedness. I gave you my solemn oath and entered into a covenant with you, declares the Sovereign Lord, and you became mine.*" Goes on to speak of Israel's continued rebellion and turning away, and then God dealing with us when He institutes a new covenant with Jerusalem in the day of her restoration. 16:59, 60 *"This is what the Sovereign Lord says: I will deal with you as you deserve, because you have despised my oath by breaking the covenant. Yet I will remember the covenant I made with you in the days of your youth, and I will establish and EVERLASTING covenant with you."*

III. Some believe the lie that they suffer because of ancestor's sins or sins committed against them, speaking of generational sins and excuses for sin such as blaming others, blaming parents, background or other factors. Victim- I am the way I am because . . . I am who I am because of . . . Ezekiel 18 speaks of these things, but In Ezekiel 18:30-32 he says

My Gift to God

"Therefore, O house of Israel, I will judge you, each one according to his ways, declares the Sovereign Lord. REPENT! Turn away from all your offenses; then sin will not be your downfall. Rid yourselves of all the offenses you have committed, and get a new heart and a new spirit. Why will you die, o house of Israel? For I take no pleasure in the death of anyone, declares the Sovereign Lord. REPENT AND LIVE!" He does not tell us to have him take it away. He tells us to turn away and to get a new heart. He does not tell us how, not yet anyway. The first step is to be WILLING to TURN AWAY . . . To GIVE IT ALL AWAY we have ACCOUNTABILITY in this as well. It is not all about God!!

IV. God Promises to bring Israel out of exile in Chapter 20 to a land of Milk and Honey, the most beautiful of lands, all He asks is that we get rid of our vile images that we have our eyes set on. What are you focused on? What are you looking at? Ezekiel 20:6, 7 *"I swore with uplifted hand to the descendants of the house of Jacob and revealed myself to them in Egypt. With uplifted hand I said to them, 'I am the Lord your God.' On that day I swore to them that I would bring them out of Egypt into a land I had searched out for them, a land flowing with milk and honey, the most beautiful of all lands. And I said to them, 'Each of you get rid of the vile images you have set your eyes on, and do not defile yourselves with the idols of Egypt. I am the Lord your God.'"*

V. Skip to where the Lord lays out what He plans to do to restore His people and be His people's shepherd. This is what He did for me . . . over and over and over again. His pursuit for me NEVER STOPPED . . . NEVER Ezekiel 34:11-16 *"I MYSELF will search for my sheep and look after them. As a shepherd looks after his scattered flock when he is with them, so will I look after MY sheep. I WILL RESCUE them from all the*

~ Notes ~ Teaching on Love through Ezekiel

places where they were scattered on a day of CLOUDS AND DARKNESS. I WILL bring them out from the nations and gather them from the countries, and I WILL bring them into their own land. I WILL pasture them on the mountains of Israel, in the ravines and in all the settlements in the land. I WILL tend to them in a GOOD pasture and the mountain heights of Israel will be their grazing land. There they will lie down in good grazing land, and there they will feed in a rich pasture on the mountains of Israel. I MYSELF WILL tend to my sheep and have them lie down, declares the Sovereign Lord. I WILL search for the lost and BRING BACK the strays. I WILL bind up the injured and strengthen the weak, but the sleek and the strong I will destroy. I WILL SHEPHERD THE FLOCK WITH JUSTICE." Any question of what he is exactly speaking about . . . look at verse 31 *"You my sheep, the sheep of my pasture, are people, and I am your God, declares the Sovereign Lord."*

VI. His promises continue on what He will do. Here He tells us how we are going to get a new heart and a new spirit that He spoke of in chapter 18. Ezekiel 36:24-36 *"For I will take you out of the nations; I WILL GATHER you from all the countries and BRING YOU BACK into your own land. I WILL SPRINKLE CLEAN WATER on you, and you WILL BE CLEAN; I WILL CLEANSE you from all your impurities and from all your idols. I WILL GIVE YOU A NEW HEART AND PUT A NEW SPIRIT IN YOU; I WILL REMOVE FROM YOU YOUR HEART OF STONE AND GIVE YOU A HEART OF FLESH. AND I WILL PUT MY SPIRIT IN YOU AND MOVE YOU TO FOLLOW MY DECREES AND TO BE CAREFUL TO KEEP MY LAWS. You will live in the land I gave your forefathers; you WILL BE MY PEOPLE, AND I WILL BE YOUR GOD. I WILL SAVE YOU from all your uncleanness. I WILL call for the grain and make it plentiful and will not bring famine upon you. I WILL increase the fruit of the trees and the crops of the field, so that you will no longer suffer disgrace among the nations because of famine. Then YOU WILL REMEMBER your evil ways and wicked deeds and you will loathe yourselves for your sins and detestable practices. I WANT you to know that I am NOT DOING this for your sake, declares the Sovereign Lord. Be ashamed and disgraced for your conduct, O house of Israel. On the day I cleanse you from all your sins, I WILL RESETTLE your towns, and the ruins will be rebuilt (what he is doing in my life now) The desolate land will be cultivated instead of lying desolate in the sight of all who pass through it. They will say "This land that was laid to waste has become like the Garden of Eden; the cities that lying in ruins, desolate and destroyed are now fortified and inhabited. Then the nations around you that remain will know that I the Lord have rebuilt what was destroyed and have replanted what was desolate. I THE LORD HAVE SPOKEN AND I WILL DO IT!"*

VII. This is how God reached me. I saw His hand working in my life, but it was not until I came to Him, humble in nature, giving every piece of me, willing to hold onto nothing. I had nothing to give Him and I was asking for nothing in return, except for forgiveness, purely from the deepest darkest parts of my heart. His journey towards us by far precedes our journey to Him. Sometimes, there is this picture of God dragging us to follow Him and it is perceived as something of a burden, that He is dragging us through the mud and the briars. But, it is not like that, it is the opposite. We drag OURSELVES thru the mire, He is there waiting for us. His is a walk of Love towards us, beckoning us to come closer. He cries for us to come to him. All we have to do is ask for forgiveness. Our responsibility is to answer His cry and to be willing. Do you love him enough to respond to his cry??? It is a parent calling out to their child . . . just as my mother did for me . . . just as my father did for me.

About The Author

Sarah McKinnis lives as a daughter of God, the Most High King, devoted to an imperfect life of harmony with her best friend, sweetheart, and husband, Adam. They live on a small farm in Birchwood, Tennessee, raising a flock of feathered babies. Sarah is a compassionate soul with a candid voice who uses the turbulence of her own story to facilitate peace to those experiencing relational brokenness. Her words ignite the truth of the hope, mercy, and unending grace in Christ for others. In the fearless honesty, humor, and wisdom of her writing and speaking, as well as in the authenticity of her relationships, she imparts truth in love. She heals in a world that is suffering.

For more information on book orders or scheduling Sarah to speak, please contact her in any of the ways below:
www.mygifttogod.com
Email: sarah@mygifttogod.com
Facebook: facebook.com/SMckinnisAuthor